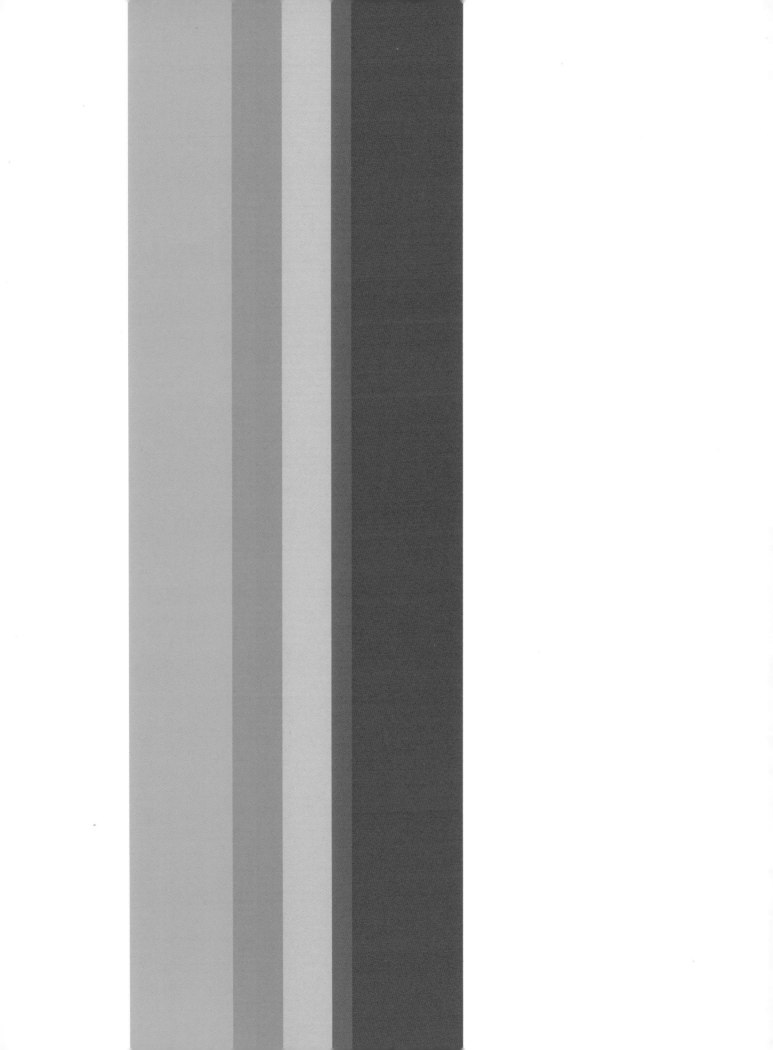

KAREN ANSON

THEIMPOSSIBLEDREAM
THE MIRACLE OF THE JASMINE MORAN CHILDREN'S MUSEUM

Foreword by David L. Boren

With Contributions by Paul Lambert

Series Editor: Gini Moore Campbell

Oklahoma Horizons Series

Printed in Canada.

ISBN 978-1-938923-04-3

Library of Congress Catalog Number 2013930369

Designed by Nathan Dunn

Dedication

This book is dedicated to the individuals, companies, and foundations that have supported the Jasmine Moran Children's Museum either through financial support, volunteerism or encouragement, and to the children who visit the Jasmine Moran Children's Museum. Their smiles make all of our efforts worthwhile.

Contents

The story which follows is truly remarkable. It is difficult to keep from thinking that it is a work of fiction, yet it is a factual account of what is possible in our society when determined and visionary leaders work with a united community to accomplish an inspired goal. This is the story of one of the largest and most visited museums for children in the United States. It is located in a town of 7,000 people, in a rural area, beyond the boundaries of any large metropolitan area.

A visit to a children's museum in Michigan with their grandchildren fostered a dream for Melvin and Jasmine Moran to build a major children's museum in Oklahoma. Within three months of their return from that visit they had called a community meeting in October of 1988 to get the project moving. Less than 20 years later the museum had been visited by families from all 50 states and 85 countries around the world. The museum recently welcomed its one-millionth visitor.

The museum opened in 1993 in a small space, in a building originally designed for an oilfield service company that had gone out of business. The museum is now housed in a multi-million dollar facility with 39,000 square feet inside and 12 acres for outside activities.

Led by the Morans and school teacher Marci Donaho, who served as board chair and later for many years as executive director, a cross section of the entire community became involved. Those who were able to do so made financial contributions, others volunteered their time, materials, skilled labor and artistic talents. Moving beyond the community they recruited state leaders to become involved and mounted a well conceived and energetically executed fundraising campaign. People of all ages became involved. Several teenagers found a new direction for their lives by becoming involved as tour guides and helpers at the museum.

A community, which was hard hit by a downturn in the energy industry, found a new sense of purpose and renewed vitality as it rallied around the idea of becoming home to a great museum which would impact the lives of thousands of children and their families.

Today, the Jasmine Moran Children's Museum in Seminole, Oklahoma, is expanding the horizons and stimulating the creative imaginations of a steady stream of visitors every week. Children form new dreams and goals for their own lives as they play out roles as judges, journalists, doctors, nurses, fire and police officers, scientists, teachers and businessmen and women in their own model town.

The history of the Jasmine Moran Children's Museum in a small Oklahoma town is not just the story of one town and its committed leaders, it is far more than that. In many ways it is an affirming story of what is possible in contemporary America.

About 175 years ago, a young Frenchman, Alexis de Tocqueville, came to America and criss-crossed the young country trying to find the source of its vitality, its strength and its greatness. He summed it up by saying that "America is great because America is good." He went on to describe America as a place where the spirit of community is unusually strong and people reach out to help each other and come together to meet shared needs. He described a process through which a leader sees a need and shares his or her idea with other neighbors. Next, they form a committee and soon work is underway to meet the goal. All of this happens without the official involvement of any government entity. The history of the Children's Museum shows that the same community spirit described by de Tocqueville in 1835 is still alive and well in America's heartland in the 21st century.

All of the children who visit the Jasmine Moran Children's Museum in the future will have many people to thank for creating such a special experience for them. In addition, all of those who read this book owe a debt to its main characters for reminding us that America remains a land where so much is possible.

— David L. Boren
from Seminole, is a former
Governor of Oklahoma and
United States Senator and
currently serves as President of
the University of Oklahoma.

The Jerusalem hotel room seemed stifling hot, although the December day was cool and the heat had been turned off to compensate for Melvin Moran's rising temperature. He felt the weakness of a high fever. His arms and legs were too heavy to move; his heart pounded so hard it seemed as though it might burst through his chest. He lay in a pool of sweat as his body burned at a temperature of 107 degrees.

Gradually, he slipped out of the conscious world and felt his spirit float to the ceiling. He looked down on his body and knew that he had died. Whatever part of him was hovering overhead felt anxious; he did not want to die. It was not that he was fearful of God or the afterlife — he was a religious man and felt secure in his faith and the good life he had led. But he had so many responsibilities that still needed his attention. He did not want to leave the family he loved, the work that consumed him and the community service that seemed to be making a real difference in the world around him. At his core, the small, love-filled man from Seminole, Oklahoma, felt there was something left to be done.

And then there was a difference in the room and Melvin felt God's presence. He was calmer now and felt brave enough to ask God to return him to life. He spoke with God for only a couple of minutes, but in that time, he told God he had unfinished business and God agreed. God asked Melvin to do something and Melvin promised; he then was returned to his bed, completely healed and ready to go out to dinner.

"I have thought about and recalled that promise hundreds of times," said Melvin Moran of that incredible day in 1981. "And that promise continues to direct what I try to do with my life."

Melvin never divulged the promise to anyone, but, at 82, says he tries to live up to it every day. Did that spiritual experience, which he said changed him in many ways, eventually lead to a glorious, golden place where children's transcendent dreams are kindled and launched sparkling like fireworks into the future?

His careful answer: Possibly.

And did the man that God smiled on that day in Jerusalem have divine help in realizing a hallowed place for nurturing children?

The people involved in building the Jasmine Moran Children's Museum believe that premise is also very likely.

Inspiration

inspiration (inspəˈrāSHən), n. an inspiring or animating action or influence: something inspired, as an idea, a result of inspired activity, a thing or person that inspires

MICHIGAN VISITORS CENTER

It was entirely by chance — or providence — that Melvin and Jasmine Moran happened upon Michigan's Children's Museum. It was August, 1988, and they were driving to Mackinac Island in Northern Michigan with their daughter and son-in-law, Marilyn Moran-Townsend and Bill Townsend, and their granddaughters, Allison, age seven, and Julie, age five.

"Mom and Dad drove a van to Fort Wayne [Indiana] to pick us up and then we drove to Mackinac," remembered Moran-Townsend. "We had an extra day to spend in Michigan prior to the start of our Mackinac reservation. When we crossed the state line between Indiana and Michigan, we stopped at a visitor's center and perused the travel brochures to find something to do.

"I spotted a brochure for a children's museum in Flint. Because I had previously taken our young daughters to the Children's Museum in Indianapolis,

I suggested we try the Flint museum. Mom and Dad agreed, although they had no idea what was in store, as neither had seen or heard of a children's museum."

The family set out for Flint, where they reserved rooms in a motel and headed to the museum.

The Flint museum was made up of 11,000 square feet in the basement of a bank, nearly a full city block in downtown Flint. When they arrived, the girls immersed themselves in the many exhibits and activities available.

"What I remember most was how excited Mom and Dad were," said Moran-Townsend. "They moved from exhibit to exhibit, saying, 'Wow!' 'What a neat idea.' 'I had no idea such a place existed.'"

In his enthusiasm, Melvin asked to speak to the museum director, who graciously answered questions about how the museum came to be and gave Melvin permission to video the facility.

Flint Children's Museum came about after a 1979 trip to Washington, D.C., by Flint educator Mary Newman. It started with a small antiques and craft exhibit in Flint's Sloan Museum. The exhibit was so popular and received so much community support that it was able to open on its own in 1986 at North Bank Center, where it operated for seven years. A large anonymous gift to the museum's endowment fund in 1990 and the donation of a building in 1993 gave the museum its permanent home at 1602 W. University Avenue.

"Dad shot tons of very jerky video," Moran-

Townsend said. "I do not believe he missed a single exhibit or sign. His video particularly focused on following Allison and Julie throughout the museum to see what captured their imagination."

Melvin saw the museum as a place for children to learn and grow. He and Jasmine said they loved watching their granddaughters interact with the exhibits, especially the ones that expanded their horizons and gave them a chance to be anyone and anything they wanted to be.

"I recall how much Allison and Julie loved to dress up and take on different roles," said Moran-Townsend, who added that at home they had an attic full of costumes. "The Flint museum enabled them to put on firefighter clothing or doctor accessories. That lit the fuse that eventually became Kids Town in the Jasmine Moran Children's Museum."

Suddenly, in both Jasmine's and Melvin's minds, blossomed full-blown the idea to build such a place in their hometown.

INSPIRATION

Predestination

predestination (pri-des-tuh-ney-shuhn), n. fate; destiny,
the state of being predestinated or predestined, an act of
predestinating or predestining

MEET THE MORANS

The spark which led to the building of the Jasmine Moran Children's Museum may have been a spur-of-the-moment visit to the Flint, Michigan, Children's Museum, but, as with any fire, conditions have to be right for ignition. Melvin's visit with God in 1981 kindled the glow of love and charity that had begun in his childhood, grew with his marriage and burned brightly with his new project. Conditions for such a project needed not only the heat of his excitement, but the breath of fresh air from his bride of 34 years.

Melvin Moran was born in St. Joseph, Missouri, on September 18, 1930, to Meyer and Elsie Fine Moran. The family lived in Maud, Oklahoma, for five years before relocating to Seminole, which Melvin always would consider his beloved hometown.

Meyer Moran, a recent Jewish immigrant from Latvia, had an oilfield junk business, which he parlayed into a successful oil company, providing a good life for his children–Melvin, Sidney and Jeannie Tiras. Meyer died in 1979. Melvin's visit to Jerusalem

Jasmine and Melvin Moran were inspired by a museum in Flint, Michigan, to build one for children in their hometown of Seminole, Oklahoma. Above, the Morans at Melvin's induction into the Oklahoma Hall of Fame in 1997.

in 1981 was to dedicate a research wing of the Ben Gurion University library in Meyer's name because of the Moran family's support of the Israeli university.

Melvin's mother, Elsie, also an Eastern Europe immigrant, was a kind and gentle woman, who watched over her children and taught them the important things in life early on.

"Melvin, you are the only Jewish child in your class and you may be the only Jewish person some of your classmates will ever meet," she often told her son as he attended school in rural Oklahoma, where Jews were definitely a minority.

"What they think about Jewish people is going to be what they think about you. You have to be good for that reason."

She taught by example, always choosing to sit in the back of the bus with the African-Americans to show her support for their civil rights.

The elder Morans personally were responsible for bringing over family member after family member, helping many to escape the Holocaust of World War II. Their charitable ways kept the Moran household full of recent immigrants, and taught their children the importance of family.

They moved to Tulsa when Melvin was in junior high so he could receive the full training for bar mitzvah, again stressing the importance of religion and family responsibility in life.

After graduation from high school at age 16, Melvin attended the University of Missouri at Columbia, graduating in 1951 with a bachelor's degree in business administration. Melvin had taken AIR-ROTC in college, so he was commissioned as a second lieutenant upon his graduation. He was assigned to the 8th Aviation Field Depot Squadron (AFDS), and for a very short time he served as an air police officer at Sandia Base in Albuquerque, New Mexico. The unit's job: loading and unloading atomic weapons. Then suddenly, in a turn of events that would forever change Melvin's life, his unit was ordered to England.

In England, Melvin served as supply officer at Lakenheath Base in England, 70 miles north of London and 20 miles from Cambridge. On frequent trips to London, Melvin met West End actress Jasmine Lindsay.

He loves to tell the story of how their meeting came about because of his relationship with a car thief. Melvin's friends had introduced him to an officer at the American Embassy in London who knew a lot of theater people in London, including the future Miss England, Lillemor Knutsen. She and Melvin dated for awhile and, according to Melvin, when she wanted to break up with him, she convinced him to call her friend, Jasmine Lindsay, for a blind date.

Later Melvin found out that the embassy officer was not an employee of the American government at all, but a con man who made his living off stealing the cars of American military members. Even that unscrupulous thief, however, could not bring himself to swindle the gentle and genuinely nice American, Melvin Moran.

Although their first blind date did not go very well, Jasmine agreed to a second date and, before long, she and Melvin were planning a return to the United States together and their wedding.

Jasmine was born in Hornchurch, Essex. Her father, a waiter on a train, died when she was four, leaving her mother with three small girls to rear. Lilian Davina MacPhee Burchell worked days at a "knick-knack shop" and nights at a bus station. She had been a championship Highland dancer and sang with a beautiful soprano voice. Sometimes she entertained at the nearby aerodrome.

"Our town was on a direct route between the ocean and London and we had an aerodrome a half mile away, which used to be a training facility," said Jasmine.

The facility drew constant bombings.

"For 18 months, we were bombed 18 or 20 times a day," Jasmine said. "We had to hurry to get to school between bombings. They would fire on anything below, including children. You would hear the bullets all around you; the sound was like a 'splat.'"

Jasmine spent much of her earliest years in a hospital with pneumonia and later scabies, with her hands tied to the bed so she would not scratch the hideous itch. She grew up dyslexic, which she said forced her to be strong. Her teachers discovered that she had a lovely singing voice.

"The teacher probably thought my loud voice could cover the sound of the bombs," Jasmine

PREDESTINATION

said, laughing. "She probably thought, 'Let's find her something she can do.' She helped decide my career."

At age 10, Jasmine auditioned and was accepted at the Italia Conti school, where Anthony Newly and other English stars began their training.

"We were as poor as church mice," Jasmine said. "My mother spoke to them and they said I could pay it out by working. I had my first West End show at age 11." West End in London is comparable to Broadway in New York.

When she met Melvin, she was 17 and performing in *Excitement*. The two dated for 18 months until his tour of duty was over and he returned to the United States.

While in *Excitement* she auditioned for a role in the new musical *South Pacific*. It had opened five months earlier and two of the women already had to leave the show. For those two parts, 200 women auditioned. After several call-backs, Jasmine was given one of the parts, which she played for 18 months.

"Jasmine will tell you that her claim to fame is that she had a larger role in the show than did Sean Connery," Melvin always joked.

Melvin went home in June of 1953 and Jasmine followed in October. She studied Judaism during her final months in England, and converted when she first arrived in New York. They were married in Tulsa on November 22, 1953. Two hundred and fifty were invited to the popular couple's wedding; 500 showed up.

Melvin started at the bottom in the family business. He moved his new bride to Seminole and

Jasmine Lindsay was a successful West End actress in London when she met Melvin Moran in 1952.

began working as a roustabout on a well-servicing unit, from 7:00 a.m. to well after dark, six or seven days a week for a salary of $300 a month, less money and fewer benefits than he took home in the military.

To Jasmine, Melvin's beloved hometown was "the bowels of the earth." She said it was populated with bootleggers and prostitutes, a statement which is backed up by a history of the town's oil boom. Jasmine immediately was pregnant and sick, and the transition to housewifery in the heat of an Oklahoma summer was not easy. The homesickness she felt was more devastating.

As the years passed, Jasmine came to love Seminole as much as her husband did. They became involved in the social life and the school. Melvin became involved in the town's politics.

In 1956 or 1957, Melvin served on a grand jury, an experience which convinced him of the need for public service.

"It was obvious to me that if good people do not become active in their community, then bad things are going to happen," Melvin said. "I wanted Seminole to be a good community in which my family and I could live and work."

In 1961, Melvin filed for an open seat on the Seminole City Council. He was elected and served seven two-year terms, never drawing an opponent.

He led his city as councilor and mayor for 18 years, serving on the Chamber of Commerce, local civic organizations and then on state boards, bi-partisan think tanks and in educational, tourism and economic advisory positions. He spoke wherever he could, encouraging people to become involved. He was successful in getting Seminole citizens to run for office, and in encouraging good ethical candidates at the state and even federal level. As a result of his involvement in politics and philanthropy, Melvin became well-known not only in Oklahoma, but nationally and internationally.

Melvin rose in his father's company and took the helm upon Meyer's death in 1979. He and Jasmine had three children, two daughters and a son, who all became kind, generous and caring people like their parents, each winning honors for their devotion to ethics and community.

"Melvin taught me about tzedakah," said Robert Henry, the Morans' friend, who currently serves as president of Oklahoma City University. "It is often translated as charity, but it is really righteousness, which encompasses justice, too. The essential point of it is that righteousness is its own reward. You do good not to get something for it but because the prophets tell you to do good. There are different levels of giving in tzedakah, levels of charity, with the highest being an anonymous donor to an anonymous donee, with no one other than God and you knowing that you are trying to do right.

"You see that in Melvin's life. He is the most dedicated person. Melvin knows how to run a business and he can almost do it on automatic pilot," Henry continued. "He does that in a half day and the rest of his day and night are spent on every good cause."

Contentplation

contemplation (kon-tuhm-pley-shuhn), n. thoughtful
observation, full or deep consideration;
reflection, purpose or intention

THE PROCESS BEGINS

The Morans were well-traveled. They had been to Israel many times, to Europe and to Canada. They had taken trips alone and with their large, extended family. But, even with all the inspirational things they had seen and done, they had never considered taking on an enterprise like building a museum.

"Oklahoma has nothing like this, but we should," said Jasmine, that day in Flint, Michigan.

"We can do this in Seminole," said Melvin.

Their daughter was not quite so sure.

"Conventional wisdom would say a world-class children's museum could not possibly be built in a town of 7,000 with a physical distance of an hour to the closest major metropolitan population," said Moran-Townsend. "Who will visit? Who will serve as volunteers? What schools will schedule field trips to such a rural destination? And what foundation would financially support such a tiny place? The answer in most cases would probably be 'no one.'"

But, as though they were on a sacred mission, Melvin and Jasmine turned away all doubt. Their faith and enthusiasm grew by leaps and bounds. They spent six hours at the museum and the next five days on Mackinac Island, accessible only by ferry, where they walked, bicycled, played with the grandchildren and dreamed about a children's museum.

The spark was struck.

For the next month, a children's museum was all the Morans could think about. They traveled to Denver, Colorado, to visit the children's museum there. They talked with economic developers and Chamber of Commerce officials in their hometown.

Bob Jones was not only one of Melvin's closest friends, but he had served as manager of the Seminole Chamber of Commerce since 1969.

"Melvin showed me this homemade video of their visit to the Flint Children's Museum," Jones said. "He told me he wanted to establish a legacy for his wife and that he was establishing a $100,000 special account to finance the startup of a children's museum."

While Jones loved Melvin and thought the museum would be an interesting project, he also had his doubts.

"The oilfield had busted in Oklahoma," he said. Oil prices went from $28 a barrel in 1985 to below $10 a barrel the next year. A study in 1986 showed the average cost of lifting a barrel of oil to the surface was $15, meaning the owners of the well lost money on every barrel.

While banks closed in Oklahoma City, Seminole faced a depression that lasted for three years. More than 150 energy firms in Seminole collapsed; 90 percent went bankrupt and out of business. Homes were for sale on every block; almost half of the downtown businesses shut down.

Melvin's own company, Moran Oil, was hit hard. They were able to keep the wells running and never had to lay off one employee, but they had to borrow money to keep the company alive.

Even so, the Morans believed Seminole needed the museum and that they had been chosen to lead the project.

"It would be a joy to the local children," Jasmine said. "We were both concerned about the latchkey children, stuck in front of the television while their parents were both working. We wanted it to be more than for the children in Seminole. We thought, if we are not going to do this, there is no point in having wealth. We have had wealthy friends who did wonderful things with their money and they were quiet with it. I always wondered why people have private jets, their own hotel rooms; we always travel coach. If you do not do good with money, then I do not know why God gave it to you.

"I tell Melvin that he made a lot of money taking something from the ground and that if you put nothing back, you have raped the earth," Jasmine said. "You can only wear so many shoes, so many pairs of pants. A life like that would drive me nuts. I did not come from it and I would not want it. Besides that, my mother would stand up in her grave and say, 'If you can not do better than that, you should just leave.'"

In a January 24, 1993, story for *The Sunday Oklahoman*, Jasmine is quoted as becoming "indignant" when people asked why they chose to build their museum in Seminole.

"This is my home," she said. "Melvin and I are very active with things in the state. We are not the Beverly Hillbillies."

Melvin was an optimist. He was sure oil prices would bounce back, and in the meantime, the project could bring the community together. But he realized that convincing Seminole civic leaders to get behind the project might be a difficult task.

"There were two groups of people we thought might embrace this idea: educators and young mothers," Melvin said. "Bob and I put together a list of fifteen people and invited them to be my guests for lunch at the Gusher Inn."

The invitation for the October, 1988, luncheon did not outline the topic for discussion as Melvin was sure no one would attend if they knew what he wanted from them. All but one of those invited responded that they would come.

The one hold-out was fourth grade teacher Marci Donaho. She had no idea why she was being invited for lunch. Instead she went to the Northwood School cafeteria along with her class. Forever afterwards, Marci would call it fate: the entrée that day was her least favorite food, the beanie-weenie special.

She was reminded of the nice lunch awaiting her at the Gusher Inn. Even more suggestive of other forces at work was the fact that on this particular day, she was actually free to leave her students to attend. As though being drawn, Marci left the cafeteria.

"I had met Marci during the Oklahoma 'Yes, Yes, Yes' campaign," Jones said. "Oklahoma was trying to pass three education questions and Marci was the spokesperson for the teachers of Seminole. She did such a fantastic job. Melvin was looking for a special person to lead the organization of the new foundation. I asked him to check with Marci. He did not know her, but talked to the superintendent about her and put her on the list."

The hand of fate continued to work as Marci attended the meeting, saw Melvin's video and agreed to be on the board. Before she left, Jones told her that he was supposed to ask her to serve as board president.

"I did not even know what I was saying 'yes' to," said the woman who would one day leave her beloved fourth graders and pledge her life to the museum. "People cannot say 'no' to Melvin. I guess it is because of his demeanor. His size is part of his charm, as well as his smile."

To Melvin, Marci became the key to the success of the museum.

"I may know a little about organization and

finance, but I know nothing about the education of children; Marci knows everything about it," he said. "If you ask Marci, she will tell you the museum was a team effort, and, of course, she is right. But Marci is the team leader."

Marci is a native of Morenci, Arizona. She has an education degree from Arizona State University, where she met her husband, Dale Donaho. With their daughter, Renáe, they moved to Norman, Oklahoma, in 1977, where Marci taught in the Moore school system and her husband worked in an oil-related business. In 1982, they moved to Seminole, where she taught third, then fourth, grade.

"I firmly believe that a higher power was involved in this museum," Marci said with certainty. "I believe we had some extra help. There was the down economy, lots of problems with the building, but everything always worked out. I feel we were meant to be here."

Marci has been a driving force in creating and later administering the project which soon became the Jasmine Moran Children's Museum (JMCM). She has been cited by many as the third person, along with the Morans, in the holy trinity of genius in the JMCM.

"Remember that Marci was an OM-er," said friends Stephanie and Jim Cook. Dr. Jim Cook was then president of Seminole State College.

"That translates to being a problem-solver, being spontaneous and creative."

They referred to Marci's time as Odyssey of the Mind (OM) sponsor at Northwood Elementary. OM is an educational program providing creative problem solving opportunities for students in grades kindergarten through college. Teams apply their creativity to solve problems, from building a mechanical device to presenting their own interpretation of literary classics. They bring their solutions to competitions at local, state and world levels. During Marci's time as OM sponsor, her teams won local and state competitions and advanced to nationals.

"A whole crew of special kids came through

our schools about that time," said the Cooks. "Because of her enthusiasm and creativity, and her involvement with OM, Marci was a natural for the museum project. She was not afraid to try something new."

Melvin took his idea to the Chamber of Commerce, Seminole Industrial Foundation and Seminole State College (SSC), generating support, and board members, along the way. Local attorney Ed Cadenhead donated office space so the board could have a place to work, an address and a telephone. A part-time director was now needed, so board member Randa Jones was hired for the position.

"We knew this thing would pan out because Melvin would just keep coming up with ideas and pursuing it," said Jim Cook, who became a member of the museum's board almost from the beginning.

"He is not the kind to say, 'This is a good idea, here is the initial money, now you guys carry on.' He has been so active from the beginning. He was so excited about this. He had so much heart in it."

A busy man himself — Cook coached baseball and soccer, was a scoutmaster and a member of the Chamber, in addition to his day job — he never thought of saying "no" to the project.

"I do not know why," he said, laughing, years later. "I must have had incredible energy back then. I thought it would be kind of fun to work with this group, and it was supposed to be just one night a month!"

He was no busier than Melvin, Cook added. "At the time that Melvin was a regent on the SSC board, he was on around 11 other boards," he pointed out.

Cook's own energy and enthusiasm drew other supporters to the project.

"I am sure that I was encouraged by President Cook to become involved with the museum," said Lana Reynolds, Seminole State College's Vice President for Institutional Advancement.

"While my work in pubic relations and institutional advancement at the college always has driven me to be involved in community affairs, some projects become a passion.

"Working side by side with people you admire so much like Melvin and Marci and with volunteers from all parts of the state on a project that helped children and helped our community, it was easy to develop a passion for the Children's Museum. It was personally rewarding and fun to be part of something good."

After a few months, Randa Jones left the part-time director position, and was followed by another board member, Tommy Mills. He agreed to accept the director's role and resigned from the board only if another man was chosen to replace him on the board. Cook was selected for the board at that time.

A few months later, Mills' position became full time. He guided the museum for the remaining portion of the creation phase and the first three years of the museum's existence. He is credited with keeping the museum supporters tightly focused on their theme and with keeping Melvin's multitude of ideas and plans on track.

"I had been at the initial luncheon," Mills said, in a 2006 interview with Paul F. Lambert. "I was asked to be on a steering committee with Marci, Teri Hooten and Randa Jones."

He admitted to being another skeptic until he researched the idea.

"I learned that, at that time, there were 40,000 kids at every grade level in Oklahoma," he said. "That is a large potential audience. Melvin thought we could get them all!"

They discussed that the museum, with Seminole's central location, would be within a two-hour drive of 70 percent of those children, which further confirmed Melvin and Jasmine's belief that Seminole was the perfect place for the Children's Museum.

Mills visited several children's museums, both in and out of Oklahoma, and read an interesting article on the Billy Graham Museum, which led to the Jasmine Moran Children's Museum having a heaven-like perspective.

"At the Billy Graham Museum, you entered a long hall that took you up, rising until you were eventually reaching two and a half floors above ground," Mills said. "Suddenly you round a corner to a big expanse; the designers wanted visitors to have the impression of going to heaven and looking down below.

"We built a smaller version of their idea. Here

you do not see into the museum until traversing a hall and rounding a corner. Then you are suddenly in Kidtown with all its colors and shapes and brick streets."

Mills said he was impressed by Silver Dollar City at Branson, Missouri, and by Disneyworld and wanted those effects for the children in Seminole. Years before his involvement with the Children's Museum, he had worked for Farmland Industries in northern Kansas and northern Iowa. In their board room was a sign that said, "Make no little plans. They have no magic to stir men's blood," a quote by Daniel Burnham (1846-1912), a Chicago architect. Mills emphasized that sentiment in the museum's planning.

"I told Melvin, 'If we are going to do this, we have to knock their socks off. We have got to make them say wow,'" Mills said, a philosophy which matched Melvin's own. "From that point on, we set out to build something so outstanding that children and parents both would be impressed." The philosophy would guarantee that visitors would want to return.

The director had his work cut out for him keeping the museum project on track and fending off the offerings of a generous, well-intentioned community.

"In the beginning the museum was given lots of things people no longer wanted," Mills said. "During the early stages we hated to turn down 'stuff.'"

"But I wanted our museum to be special. It was

going to have to support itself as much as possible and we found we could get significant funding for the approach we finally chose," Mills said.

Mills hired Ann Biddy to be the museum's second employee. For about four years before the museum opened, and a year after she was responsible for the museum's bookkeeping.

"I love a project, so I loved working at the museum and I am very proud to have been a part of it," Biddy said 20 years later.

At first she and Mills were the only paid employees. She worked five half-days each week.

"There was not much payroll to be done,

Ann Biddy, left, was hired as bookkeeper by the Museum's first director, Tommy Mills, right.

but Tommy was working on grants and I helped him," Biddy said. "Our offices were upstairs, but as the project began to unfold, I would have to go downstairs and see what was going on. It was exciting to watch. And going up and down all those stairs kept me in very good shape," she laughed.

"The budget was very tight. I remember once when there was not enough money to pay the quarterly taxes, which were not very much, because we did not have much money coming in. Every time we needed money, we had to go to Melvin and he always gave us whatever we needed. But I felt so bad to go to him, because in those times, oil was not $100 a barrel.

"The budget did not grow that much while I was there," Biddy continued. "Most of the money that came in was earmarked for a project and there was not that much coming through the front door or gift shop. The utilities and overhead on that big building cost a lot. Melvin continued to support the museum the whole time I was there."

Strict records were kept, she said, and annual audits were done by John Gibson, a certified public accountant from Shawnee. The 1989-1990 operating budget was $150,800.

Melvin came to the museum every day, Biddy remembered, with his list of things he would like to see done, and to make sure they had followed up on his suggestions.

"He was always positive and enthusiastic," she said.

The executive committee was also a huge help.

"Harry Coates, Marci, Jim Cook...they always took the time to come by and talk to us if we had any problems," she said.

Biddy often brought her daughter, Lauren, to work, leaving her in the area that soon became the Tot Spot while she finished up her work.

So diligent was Biddy that on May 8, 1992, on the way to the hospital to deliver her son, Brent, she stopped off at the museum to do payroll.

"Well, I could not leave when people were waiting to be paid," she said. "Maybe I paid a few

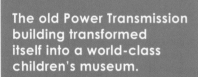

The old Power Transmission building transformed itself into a world-class children's museum.

bills, too, while I was there."

Brent was born that afternoon.

"I think I took off a whole week," she said.

Led by the format Bob Jones had used with the Chamber of Commerce, the new board adopted bylaws, an article of incorporation and applied for a tax exemption from the Internal Revenue Service and the State of Oklahoma. The applications immediately were accepted on April 14, 1989. The next order of business was to find a building.

"There were several buildings downtown, but we could not find the right size," Jones said. They considered the TS&H building at Broadway and Milt Phillips and the Curry Hardin Furniture building at 301 N. Milt Phillips. But neither seemed big enough, and then Jones noticed the former Power Transmission building at 1714 SH 9 West.

Power Transmission was one of the oilfield-related businesses that had gone bankrupt during the oil bust. The almost-new, 20,000 square-foot building and its seven and a half acres were in the hands of the mortgage company, American National Bank of Shawnee. The price of $300,000 seemed reasonable. Melvin agreed to the asking price, then requested that the bank make a donation. They donated $31,750 and Seminole had a facility for a world-class children's museum. Bank President Jerry Lanier was instrumental in working out arrangements for the purchase.

While still in very good condition, the Power Transmission building had been used to repair engines for drilling rigs. Oil and grease filmed every surface. The energy and enthusiasm of the new team was such that they decided to clean it themselves.

"We did not have money to hire someone," Marci pointed out.

So the first of a series of work nights was scheduled for June 20, 1989. It must have been inspiring to see a college president cleaning windows, academic doctorates scraping floors, a former actress cleaning oil from troughs and oilfield tycoons tearing out chain link fencing and pulling up concrete blocks.

"It started with a crowd, but it soon got down to a small bunch of people," said Jim Cook. "We all had to chip in to get it presentable. We scraped those red vinyl tiles up off the concrete floor in the front office where they used to come to have their trucks serviced.

"Marie Dawson and I cleaned the big windows, inside and out. I am sure we did a crummy job – you know how Marie gets distracted!"

Dale Donaho, Marci's husband, was pulling electrical conduit from the walls when sparks flew. Although the electricity had been turned off, one line had not been killed.

"But we had fun," he said. They ordered pizza and made it a party.

"We all said we were going to think about it twice next time Melvin invited us to a party," said board member Donna Hardin.

Even Melvin and Jasmine joined the work,

Jasmine slipping and sliding across the floor and cleaning up oil.

"We were not a large board then," Marci remembered. "Zora and Jim Fowler, Dale and myself, Cai Levy, Vicki Moran, Teri Hooten, Kathy Jett Ridgeway."

Dr. James Fowler, a professor at Seminole State College, was invited to join the project, so his wife, Zora Fowler, became involved, as well.

"When the first work session was scheduled, we both arrived ready for physical labor," Zora Fowler said. "It was almost impossible to walk through that building that was obviously made for other purposes, and to be able to see the future of the museum — but I am so glad someone had the vision! What I remember the most about that day were the pits in the floor that were filled with oil and dirt from trucks, and trying to shovel that gunk."

"We developed a lot of camaraderie," said Lana Reynolds.

As the group of museum planners got ready for their first board meeting, Vicki Moran Horton, an interior designer and Melvin's niece, cut out silhouettes of cardboard to depict kids with scissors, crayons and paints, blowing bubbles, playing hospital.

"We were going to have a meeting here and we wanted people to have an idea what the museum would be like," Marci said.

"It sure did not look then like any place where kids would ever be playing — unless they wanted to play in oil pits," said Cai Levy, a member of the group which was always afterward referred to as "the design team."

"I remember that it was summer and it was so hot. . . but we had a deadline. We needed to build morale, make people excited about the project," Levy continued.

They painted handprints over everything. They used all their children and their own handprints, and even Jasmine and Melvin's. They knew that, later, the walls and murals would cover the handprints. Even today, those who worked on the museum before it was a museum sometimes like to think of all the handprints of those creative, caring people still there, somewhere, deep in the hidden places of the museum.

At the first board meeting in the new facility, the items left on the shelves by Power Transmission were auctioned off to raise capital. But everyone involved knew they were going to need a lot more money than that, and a lot of luck.

The design team included local artists Cai Levy, Teri Hooten, Kathy Jett Ridgeway and Vicki Moran. *Courtesy C.J. Vigil.*

Collaboration

collaboration (kuh-lab-uh-rey-shuhn), n. to work, one with
another; cooperate, the act or process of collaborating;
a product resulting from collaboration

PLANNING A MUSEUM

"Before we could fundraise, we needed to plan the museum," Melvin said, "but there are no manuals on how to create a children's museum."

"We certainly knew nothing about designing or fabricating exhibits," Marci said. "In fact, we had no idea what we were doing. We just wanted to build something special for kids. We frequently came to forks in the road and had to make major decisions. We did not make these decisions from experience or knowledge, for we had neither.

"Yet every decision we made seemed to have been the right decision. We do not believe that this 'just happened,'" she continued. "We truly believe that God wanted this special place for children created and that he guided us every step of the way."

That day back in October, 1988, before the group left the Gusher Inn, Marci had been named president of the board, Tommy Mills was named vice president and Randa Jones, secretary-treasurer.

"I agreed to chair the fundraising committee only because no one else would do it," said Melvin.

"We had a president with no leadership experience and a fundraiser with no fundraising experience," Marci joked.

"I had an aversion to asking anyone for money for anything," Melvin said. "I even refused to go with my daughters when they were selling Girl Scout cookies. But I knew the project would go nowhere if we did not have someone to do the fundraising."

So, our intrepid but angelic museum-builder, facing one of the biggest challenges of his life, set out to find financing for his dream. Melvin's original plan was to compose a letter and send it to 200 potential donors.

"I assumed we would have the money to construct the museum in two weeks and would probably be open in six months," Melvin said.

But Nancy Anthony, executive director of the Oklahoma City Community Foundation, explained the error of his thinking.

"She told me I would be lucky to raise enough money to pay for the stamps with that plan," Melvin said. "She said you have to go to people you know. I have been on a lot of boards, so I am able to open doors."

Melvin, acting on her brilliant advice, wrote

instead to 24 prominent Oklahomans, people he knew and who he believed would provide the credibility he needed; and, as board members, they would open other doors.

The first letter he sent was to David and Molly Boren, asking them to serve on the museum's advisory board. Melvin had known David Boren when the former governor and United States Senator was growing up in Seminole, and had served as David's campaign chairman. The Borens' positive response generated others.

"The response we received from Alex Adwan [former Seminole resident employed at that time as an editorial page editor of the *Tulsa World* newspaper] was typical," Marci said. "He wrote, 'I do not know what a children's museum is, but I would be honored to serve on any board with David and Molly Boren.'"

"No one can tell Melvin 'no', so he succeeded in bringing together the brightest and most effective leaders in our state," said Betty Price, former director of the Oklahoma Arts Council. "I have been fortunate to work with a board of directors at the Oklahoma Arts Council and know that the work of Melvin's board stands tall."

Although almost everyone joined, many later expressed their early doubts that the museum ever would open.

"I was the original skeptic," said Gene Rainbolt, Melvin's friend and CEO of BancFirst. "Nobody but Melvin could have succeeded in that project.

I would not have had the nerve to take it on."

"When he came to talk to me about the museum, in my mind I was saying, 'This is never going to work; there is no way this can work,'" said Robert Henry, former federal judge and now president of Oklahoma City University. "But I cannot tell Melvin that. I cannot not help him, even though I know we will both go down in flames.

"I do not think I have ever been so wrong. I was feeling bad about my lack of faith on this until four or five of the others said they felt the same way," Henry continued. "They did not think it would succeed either, but we love Melvin Moran and could not tell him 'no.' We were prepared to go off the cliff with him. He is just a visionary."

Henry, like every other person Melvin asked, made every call he was asked to make, talked to everybody he was supposed to, and did everything he could to make Melvin's dream come true.

Of the 24 well-known Oklahomans that Melvin asked to serve on an advisory board, 22 said yes. Their name recognition, like his, smoothed the way many times. In addition to those named, the list included Keener Oil Company CEO Dewey Bartlett Jr.; Congressman Mickey Edwards; Mary Frates of the Oklahoma Arts Institute; Oklahoma Supreme Court Justice Rudolph Hargrave; former state Director of Finance Alexander Holmes; former Lt. Governor Robert S. Kerr III; District Judge Gordon Melson; U.S. Senator Don Nickles; former Governor George Nigh; Supreme Court Chief Justice Marian Opala; former

Tulsa Mayor Rodger Randle; Federal Judge Frank H. Seay; former Congressman Wes Watkins and his wife Lou Watkins; and Ronald White, well known cardiologist and co-founder of the Oklahoma Heart Hospital.

"The majority became active, doing fundraisers like celebrity golf tournaments," Melvin said. "Most are donors as well. As for the original Seminole board members, we later decided the board should reflect a state focus. Now there are 125 members from all over Oklahoma, all creative people. When we ask for a grant, it is helpful to show that these well-known, respected people believe in our project."

Board meetings were scheduled on a monthly basis and directors would drive to a variety of cities for a dinner and business meeting. At each, Melvin introduced everyone in the room from memory, with no notes or reminders to rely on.

"Creativity is a good description for the work of the board," said Betty Price. "Fundraising was paramount and Melvin and Marci were a terrific team, along with the board of directors. Their leadership and the dedicated board members became the driving force to build a museum rivaling any in the nation.

"The friendship that developed among all concerned with the museum was remarkable," she continued.

Melvin believed that, to attract families from long distances, the museum must be something special; the organizers, agreeing with his philosophy, decided to make it the best in the country. The board organized seventeen committees, with each assigned to come up with an exhibit.

"We sat around that long table at the Chamber," said Cai Levy. "There were different people with different perspectives. Business people looked at the museum from their angle and we young mothers looked at it from the angle of small children. We bounced things off each other."

"The committees were comprised of local dedicated and creative geniuses," Marci said. "Each committee was assigned a different area, such as art, energy, aeronautics, medicine, firefighting and so on. These committees came up with exhibit ideas and when the ideas were accepted by the board, the committees' tasks were to design the exhibits."

Kathy Jett Ridgeway's committee studied aeronautics. They looked into a flight simulator, a cockpit with a tape recording of communication from pilot to ground crew, flight suits and videos from the pilot's perspective, with the illusion of flying projected onto a wall. They also explored a vertigo chamber, weather charts for plotting itineraries, space flight videos of astronauts walking on the moon, a moon rock and an astronaut suit on a mannequin.

Julia Ewert helped with the Recreation Committee. They considered a carousel, a room for playing in a ball pit, and an area with lots of climbing and mazes. Water and sand tables, a sports center with a basketball goal and batting cages were debated. An area to play with blocks or Legos, an outdoor camping area, and an outdoor play space with a rope "spider," shuffle board, hopscotch and playhouse were discussed.

Jonna Bunyan's Visual Arts Committee located double-sided elementary school-sized art easels for $81 each, to be placed in an arts and crafts area. They talked about distortion mirrors as another aspect of their exhibit.

Also on the Visual Arts Committee was Marie Dawson, who talked to several artists about painting murals for the museum. She talked to Oklahoma City's KOCO Channel 5 about acquiring television studio equipment. Gary Wood at Channel 5 told her they had several items stored that they might be able to donate.

Mac Carter and the Transportation Committee worked on locating a railroad caboose and an F-14 aircraft on which children could climb. They had discussed with a Shawnee collector a display of antique cars, but realized that access would have to be restricted due to the value of the vehicles.

Someone had seen an old model of the Beverly Hillbillies truck that had been donated to the School of the Ozarks; it was suggested they look for something like that as well.

Ideas for outdoor exhibits included a military jeep or ambulance, things which often were available through State Surplus Properties. A police car with uniforms and a steam engine also were discussed.

Lana Reynolds and the Communications Committee considered implementing the front pages of the *Tulsa World*, walkie talkies, a newspaper exhibit by Gannett Company Inc., a teleprompter, cameras, a recording studio, soundproof booths with headphones to listen to recorded music, and instruments.

Niki Merrill and the Consumerism and Math Committee discussed a grocery store with shopping carts, pretend food, shelves, scales for fruits and vegetables, scanners and check-out counters. They searched for a meat counter, refrigerator case and produce bins.

They also considered setting up a bank, with Plexiglas tubes for sending deposits to tellers, change drawers, calculators, security guards, money bags and a safe. Math would be incorporated into each of the two areas.

Zora Fowler and the Computer Science Committee decided on Apple equipment because of the color graphics and the amount of software available for the target age group. They planned to use Muppet software with separate alphabetically lettered keyboards for small children.

Tommy Mills said the Agriculture Committee would center around food production, with perhaps a farm tractor. Seed and agriculture companies would be contacted for sponsorships.

Bonnie Lee Grisso worked on the Medical Science Committee. They considered a hospital setting with a bed, tray, wheelchair and crutches.

They wanted a doctor's office with a stethoscope, examining table and skeleton. In a lab, they might include a microscope, x-rays and light boards for viewing them. For the vision and hearing impaired awareness exhibit they considered a Braille alphabet, blindfold, cane, language chart, audiometer, a timeline following medical history, pupil dilating machine and a tone memory machine.

Cai Levy and retired teacher Nathylee Whitley chose the Science Committee.

"We pursued all sorts of ideas in earth sciences," Levi said in a 2006 interview with Paul Lambert. "I found an exhibit with bees where you could see inside the hive. I talked to a beekeeper in Ada. We went to Platt National Park [now Chickasaw National Wildlife Refuge] in Sulphur to learn about nature.

"I got in touch with the Department of Wildlife Conservation and discovered a matching grant for a native fish aquarium. We visited various aquariums and found that the smallest freshwater fish in the United States is in McCurtain County — a pygmy sunfish."

Other ideas included a petting zoo with the hopes that a 4-H or Boy Scout group would agree to care for the animals, an exhibit on how animals had evolved and an archaeology exhibit with an imitation cave and dinosaur dig.

Levy said they all came back with their findings and found they had more exhibits than they could ever use.

COLLABORATION

"Some were not hands-on," she said, and were stored or returned to the donors.

It was then that they decided to come up with a unifying theme and the idea was pitched to the design team: Cai Levy, Teri Hooten, Vicki Moran Horton and Kathy Jett Ridgeway. They were a group of "twenty-somethings," all with children about the same age and all interested in art.

"Cai and I were pregnant at the same time and lived two houses down from each other," Hooten said. Levy and Horton had family relationships with Melvin.

Horton, Melvin's niece, was eminently qualified for the task of serving with the design team. A Los Angeles transplant, she was an interior decorator and designer, and currently was operating her own children's furniture business in Seminole, Squiggles and Dots. The company was featured in *Better Homes and Gardens* more than a dozen times and was on the cover of *Child* and *Parents* magazines. She recently had redesigned the Arts Council building, the hospital in Seminole and a local medical clinic.

"I used to visit a covered shopping mall called Old Town Mall in L.A.," Horton recalled. "Each storefront looked like it was part of a town." From this came the museum's small town concept.

"Carnival themes, cowboy/Midwest themes, animal themes, geometric themes and cartoon themes were among the original proposals," stated the design team's proposal to the board in

December, 1989.

"All these were appealing to children and lent themselves to creative architecture, design and color. However, the issues of continuity, of displaying exhibits with common topics in close physical proximity, was not easily resolved within the constraints of these themes. The problem then became one of selecting a theme that allowed exhibits with 'common threads' to be grouped together."

The committee wanted to incorporate exhibits into "clusters" of common themes by creating a "pint-sized" world of everyday experiences.

"A little research revealed that the idea of 'clustering' was not a unique one," the proposal stated. "The Cleveland Children's Museum developed the concept of exhibit clusters after observing the learning patterns displayed by children and parents in museums around the country.

"They [Cleveland Children's Museum] concluded that since learning can happen in various ways and through several sequences, we must create within the exhibits a range of learning opportunities," the design team's proposal stated.

So the design team proposed a child-sized town where children would role-play at multiple career choices. An adjoining "woods" would allow for recreation and science exhibits.

The design team also dealt with the museum's color scheme.

"Color and its affect on the human psyche is

a useful tool for influencing and stimulating children and adults, and is used in education, marketing and psychology," the proposal stated.

"For example, red is energetic and competitive; yellow is social, communicating and expressive. Orange is a high energy, focused color and blue is calming and imaginative."

"We wanted to tie the exhibits into classroom curriculum," Marci said. "Basically we were building learning centers."

To promote the project, Melvin needed something that supporters could visualize. He asked his daughter, Marilyn Moran-Townsend, and her company CVC Communications of Fort Wayne, Indiana, to make a promotional video.

"The first video, of course, contained lots of drawings to illustrate what the museum could become," Moran-Townsend said. "It did not have visuals of the actual museum since it was not yet a reality."

They used clips from Melvin's "jerky" video in Flint and his subsequent visit to the Denver Children's Museum to show what a children's museum was.

"My camera ability was terrible," Melvin admitted. "It was up and down and jerky. Marilyn described it as 'it looks like a video a child would do.'"

That idea grew into a plan to make the promotional video from a child's perspective. They used children shooting movie cameras, along with footage from Melvin's original film, and the end result became a very effective fundraising tool.

In planning the museum, the organizers had visited museums nationwide, including Oklahoma Christian College's Enterprise Square in Oklahoma City. Now Oklahoma Christian University, the attraction taught about free enterprise.

Melvin and Mills visited with President Dr. J. Terry Johnson for advice; he told them he had a model made of the various sections of Enterprise Square so possible donors could see the projected completion of the museum. The Seminole planners decided to do the same.

"We did some drawings showing various exhibits we had planned," Melvin said. "We took the drawings to the University of Oklahoma College of Architecture and they made us a model showing the exhibits in miniature, with miniature kids throughout. The size of it was such that it would fit into the trunk of a car."

With his governing board in place, his theme decided and a scale model and promotional video in hand, Melvin was now ready to take his fundraising show on the road.

COLLABORATION

Cooperation

cooperation (koh-op-uh-rey-shuhn), n. an act or instance of working or acting together for a common purpose or benefit; joint action; willingness to cooperate

FUNDRAISING BEGINS

It was not long before Melvin's groundwork began to pay off — sometimes in ways that seemed almost supernatural.

To show his promotional video, Melvin purchased a television/video cassette recorder to carry with him to presentations. Back in 1989, not every office had a DVD player.

"I wanted to make certain that our potential donors could see the video well, so we purchased a large TV/VCR," Melvin said. "It was so large the trunk of my car would not close and we had to tie it down."

The first target audience for the presentation was the Kerr-McGee Corporation in Oklahoma City, where Melvin had friends.

"The nearest parking place I could find was three blocks away," he remembered. "Somehow I manhandled the TV/VCR out of my trunk and carried it, three steps at a time, with a rest period in between, all the way."

Once there, he was told they already had expended their giving budget for that year.

"But Kerr-McGee Vice President Tom McDaniel looked at the video I brought and then said, 'Tell us how Kerr-McGee can help you,'" Melvin said. "They generously gave the project $10,000, which was our first corporate donation."

The museum board chose to use the first donation to purchase a robot, which they found in the shop of an "electronics genius" in Dallas, Texas. The robot was used not only as an exhibit, but as a fundraiser. "Kermie" was a huge hit wherever he showed up. He could walk, talk and raise his arms. Kermie also visited several Kerr-McGee functions, always to the delight of the crowd.

Museum board member David Hargis was the voice of Kermie and kids loved him. Later, when the museum opened, Hargis would look out onto the main floor of the museum from a second floor office window, from where he controlled Kermie. Hargis' voice was projected through an electronic device to make it sound robot-like. From below, the window appeared to be part of a bus mural. Hargis would watch the children from that vantage point and could interact with them in a realistic and natural way.

"But Kermie kept breaking down," said Cai Levy.

After Melvin's exhausting experience lugging the big TV/VCR unit, he needed to find another way to make his presentations. Kerr-McGee was the last

Melvin and Jasmine Moran introduce themselves to Kermie, the museum's first exhibit, made possible by a donation from Kerr-McGee Corporation. *Courtesy Jacklyn Patterson Photography.*

The kids loved Kermie, but he kept breaking down and finally was retired. *Courtesy Jacklyn Patterson Photography.*

COOPERATION

excursion for the big TV; the next week they bought a smaller one. And with the Kerr-McGee name in their pocket, other doors opened.

At the time, Melvin was a newly appointed regent on the board of Seminole State College. He knew the chairman of the Board of Regents, Frank Seay, father of the now-retired federal judge with the same name, and he knew that the elder Seay was a member of the Sarkeys Foundation board, one of the most respected philanthropic foundations in Oklahoma. Melvin asked the chairman if he thought Sarkeys might donate to the museum project. Seay said he thought they might and asked Melvin to write him a letter describing the project.

"I had been told that one simply does not ask a foundation for help, but must ask for a specific dollar amount," Melvin said. The board had hired a consultant to prepare a list of prospects and to advise them on how much they should request from each. They were told that if they thought a prospect would give $50,000, they should not ask for $5,000. Similarly, if they thought they might get $5,000, they should not ask for $50,000. When Melvin asked Seay how much to request, he was told to ask for $10,000.

But before Melvin could write the letter, the elderly Seay died. Later, Melvin related this story to another member of the museum's advisory board and was told there was another Sarkeys Foundation board member with Seminole ties — attorney Richard Bell.

Although Melvin never had met Bell, he

called and was invited to chat about the project at the Faculty House in Oklahoma City. Marci accompanied Melvin to the meeting and found Bell to be receptive to their plan. When Melvin was asked how much the museum should ask for, Bell suggested $150,000.

"He told me that most requests are reduced by half and that he thought Sarkeys might give us $75,000," Melvin said. And sure enough, they did and became the museum's first foundation donor. The money was used as seed money to begin the museum.

The Mabee Foundation turned down the museum's first request for $180,000, but a year later offered a $250,000 challenge grant for the construction and creation of the museum. The museum had to raise $1.5 million to meet the challenge, a feat they managed in one year and one month, by using the Sarkeys Foundation's donation, and contacting many other foundations, corporations and individuals. As the one-year deadline approached, and with the match not quite complete, the Mabee Foundation board extended the deadline by one month. The museum board was successful in meeting the goal.

Sometime during the first years of planning and building, Mills learned of a service organization called The Support Center [Oklahoma Center for Nonprofits]. With offices in Oklahoma City and Tulsa, the organization, itself a non-profit, had as its primary goal assisting other non-profits. They held seminars and workshops that covered everything: fundraising, human resources, non-profit management, computer use and public relations. The Center's co-founder and director was Pat Potts, who happened to be a close friend of the Morans.

"I enrolled in a number of their programs and one of the most useful was fundraising," Mills said.

"In it, besides the Center's staff, guests from corporations and foundations detailed what they expected in grant requests. In that session, I picked up a lot of information that helped us in the early fundraising. Our written applications and requests became more focused and detailed and less generalized, in the exact format the potential donor organizations expected."

Up to the time of the museum's opening, Melvin

Co-founder Melvin Moran and longtime Executive Director Marci Donaho have worked together for the betterment of the museum for more than 20 years, always giving the other credit for their success. *Courtesy Karen Anson.*

and Mills, with Marci still teaching at Northwood, engaged in a serious fundraising blitz. Both were new at the game, but as time passed, both became proficient and had great success.

Once the museum opened, it became harder for Mills to get away, but it became easier to describe an existing entity that began gaining acceptance and credibility rapidly.

"Soon we had impressive videos and attendance records to help sell the museum to donors," Mills said. "And with a living, breathing children's museum, we were able to generate a lot of coverage from the media. All the Oklahoma City television stations gave us good coverage and the print media began featuring our project."

Melvin and Marci also continued their fundraising presentations, each always giving the other the credit for their success.

"I cannot imagine the museum without Marci's leadership," Melvin said 20 years later. "She has been an integral part of our fundraising effort. Her passion [for the museum] and her love for children both sell the museum. Jasmine and I are known as the museum's co-founders. Marci should also be named as a co-founder. From the very beginning, she has been either the board president or the executive director. Her fingerprints are on every inch of the museum."

"Melvin is in my office every day, but he does not interfere with operations," Marci said. "I know I am blessed to be working with the people I do. I hear such horror stories and I am ever so grateful for this board, staff and Melvin.

"We make a great team," she said. "This is not a one-person show. It would be hard to replicate this team."

While both give each other credit, both also say there seemed to be some other driving force.

"There were just times when it seemed that everything went too smoothly," Marci said. "Things that should not have happened did."

Were those the times that Melvin's secret angel was directing their course? Melvin thinks so.

"Marci and I, while speaking to various groups about the museum, have frequently said that we thought that G-d wanted the museum to be built," said the man who had had a personal chat with that God eight years earlier, a man who made a promise to God that he never divulged, the promise that continues to direct his life to this day.

Melvin, in the way of most devout Jews, always refrains from speaking or spelling the name of God.

"There were literally hundreds of times during the creation of the museum that we came to a crossroads and had to make a decision whether to turn left or right," he said.

"And it seems like we made the correct decision every time. Marci and I have always felt that we had help from above as we made those decisions."

Several stories Melvin told lent credence to this belief.

Once, upon arriving before a foundation board to request funding, Melvin was met by a board member who hugged him and said how nice it was to see him again.

Anyone who knows Melvin is aware that he never forgets a name or a face. His memory is so legendary that friends watch in awe when he introduces 100 people at a banquet, never forgetting a name, an occupation, a spouse or a child.

But on this occasion, Melvin drew a blank. He did not remember ever having met the board member, but covered his embarrassment by responding, "Yes, wonderful to see you again, too."

During the presentation, the board member interrupted several times, saying things like, "You can believe anything Melvin tells you," and making comments about what a good person Melvin was.

The museum got the very large grant and later Melvin tried to find out how he might have known the board member, but to no avail. He found out the name of the company the board member worked for, but it was an energy company Melvin had never heard of. None of his friends in the oil community had ever heard of the company either and it was not listed in the oil directory.

The board member was one of the first to show up when the museum opened years later, and got a personal tour from Melvin along with thanks for his part in getting the grant.

"There is no doubt in my mind that we received the grant because of this board member's encouragement and comments," Melvin said. He found that the man had only been on the board for 30 days before Melvin's presentation, and that he died soon after the museum opened.

"I honestly am not sure if he actually existed," Melvin said. "Yes, he was at my fundraising presentation, but I really am not certain at all if he really really really was a person.

"But if this foundation had not given us this huge grant, I am not certain if the museum would ever have opened," Melvin said. "I continue to wonder if he and I had really known each other, or if G-d had sent him to help us."

Even the story of the grant received from the Robert S. and Grace Kerr Foundation seems to show that there was more at work during those fundraising presentations than Melvin's charm and persuasiveness.

With his new small TV/VCR in tow, Melvin and Marci approached Kerr Foundation Executive Director Dr. Anne Morgan.

"I do not have a TV at home," she said. "I do not watch TV. I am not going to watch TV here in my office. You may not plug it in. You will have to tell me about your project."

Melvin was taken aback. He fumbled through a description of a children's museum and, upon leaving the office, was sure there was no chance they would get a grant from the Kerr Foundation.

But a month later they received a check for $10,000.

"About a year later, Anne was a speaker at a fundraising seminar we attended at Fountainhead Lodge," Melvin said. "She told us that, when she went to the trustees of her foundation, she said, 'I do not think there is any chance this museum will ever open, but let's give them $10,000 for having the guts to try.'"

Once again, the museum had been the recipient of unexpected good luck.

Another time that a strange twist of fate brought a significant donor to the museum was when a friend of Melvin's resurfaced after 50 years.

Donna Pollock Terry, who had been one of Melvin's first friends when he was a child in Seminole, had moved to California in eighth grade. She worked as a professional artist, doing ads for many major companies. One day she was cleaning out an address book and came across their other grade school friend, Joe Snider.

Snider was a lawyer in Oklahoma City and answered the phone when Donna called the number to make sure it was no longer in service before she threw it out. The number was for his home and he just happened to be at home on this day, instead of at work. They renewed their friendship and Snider invited her to Oklahoma. When she came a year later, they decided to drive to Seminole to see Melvin and their old stomping grounds.

"It was astounding to me!" Terry said. "Every other kid had left. There were not that many opportunities in Seminole. The town had gone downhill after the oil boom. Melvin and his family were very, very bright people with a lot of strength and the ability to go wherever they wanted. That they stayed in Seminole, where there were no Jews that I knew of, was amazing. That he had married this beautiful showgirl and brought her here...well, we had a very sophisticated way of life in San Francisco, so I could imagine what this lovely woman gave up in coming here."

Terry does not remember what she expected of Melvin's showgirl wife, but found her to be warm and friendly. Melvin, Terry said, was "the same old Melvin."

Snider had filled her in on the museum project and Melvin, of course, wanted to take them to see it. When she saw the new museum, it was a large empty warehouse.

"Melvin told us about his dream," Terry said. "At no time did he ever say anything about money. He had his first exhibit, a robot, but it was not working yet. The more Melvin and Jasmine talked about the dream, the more I thought, 'I cannot believe he stayed. He could have gone anyplace. He has kept this town alive. And this project reflects his love of this place.'"

As the group was leaving, Terry and her husband, Ivan, trailed behind.

"My husband said, 'Let's put something towards this project,'" she said. "So we wrote a check and gave it to Melvin and he was so surprised. I think he was also proud that we believed in the project, too. I remember that he said, 'God bless you.'

"I have heard a thousand people say those words, but I still cry when I think of the way he said it."

Being part of the museum kept the Terrys close to the Morans. They asked Snider to keep them updated on the project. Later, when they saw how beautiful the museum was, they decided to leave their estate to it.

"We do not have any children or family to leave it to and we were going to leave it to the Oakland Zoo because they did not have a house big enough for the elephant," Terry said. "But later we decided the city would take care of the animals... and they have since built a bigger house for the elephant. So we redid our will and left everything to the museum."

In 1998, the Terrys were invited back for recognition. They were the guests of honor at a banquet at Seminole State College.

"It was a big affair with Senator Boren and a federal judge to thank all the donors for what they had done," Terry said. "Now here is the thing about Oklahomans and it is such a radical contrast from our environment in San Francisco — Oklahomans love each other. They take care of each other. They honor each other."

At the banquet Robert Henry began making the announcement of the donor of the year.

"He described this couple who had left everything to the museum and we realized he was talking about us," Terry said. "He brought out a big plaque and invited us up to the podium.

"I was dumb-founded, speechless," she said. "Well, I tried to make a speech, but I screwed it all up and I have spent the rest of my life wishing I could have said what I would have said, if I had had time to prepare.

Donna Pollock Terry was a childhood friend of Melvin Moran and moved to California as a child. But when she and her husband, Ivan, first learned about the Children's Museum, they knew they wanted to be a part of something so special, and bequeathed their estate to the museum. Ivan Terry died in 2011.

"I would have said, 'When we were children in Seminole, we had nothing like this museum. We had the movie theater, stamp collecting, and play. How much our lives would have been enriched if we had known what was out there for us. Now the children of Oklahoma have the Jasmine Moran Children's Museum.'

"How much more will their lives be because of it?"

To Terry, "Melvin's dream" is not like most children's museums.

"This one is not a play place," she said. "It is a place where children can experience being a doctor or a lawyer or whatever, so they can be a part of what the world will be. In the medical part, they walk on crutches, see what it is like to be blind, or live your life in a wheelchair. When we were kids, we made fun of people in wheel chairs! The museum teaches them to respect one another. A child learns while playing and that is why it was so inspiring to us."

When the brick street fundraiser was announced later, the Terrys bought a brick for everyone they knew.

"We honored our friends, our doctors, people who would never come here or know that we had honored them," she said. "I think it is beautiful that the bricks are the color of the Oklahoma soil."

The Terrys' honor was commemorated with a plaque in the museum that reads:

Donna and Ivan Terry were honored with a plaque in the museum for their contributions.

"THE WORLD ENDURES ONLY
FOR THE SAKE OF
THE BREATH OF SCHOOL CHILDREN."
The Talmud

IN HONOR OF
DONNA & IVAN TERRY

*Philanthropists & Friends
of the Jasmine Moran Children's Museum*

Presented October 23, 1998

Creation

CREATI

creation (kree-ey-shuhn), n. the act of producing or causing to exist; the act of creating; something that is or has been created

BUILDING A MUSEUM

With the money beginning to flow, it was time to begin the construction phase of the Morans' dream and, again, the forces of good seemed to provide whatever help the museum needed.

Four contractors applied for the job of construction manager. Local contractor Keith Shaw was working on the Colclazier law offices when Marci's husband, Dale Donaho, asked him to cast his hat in the ring as well. The two men had gotten to know and respect each other at a Baptist men's retreat.

"I said, 'What's a children's museum?'" Shaw remembered. "Dale told me a little and that Melvin and Jasmine were involved. I was experienced with these people and knew I would like to work with them."

"We thought we had picked one of the four applicants when Dale said we should consider Keith," said Marci. "After that, it was a no-brainer."

From the museum's beginning through the next 20 years, Seminole contractor Keith Shaw, center, has spent many hours poring over plans with museum director Marci and husband Dale. *Courtesy Karen Anson.*

"Keith is the kind of guy who wants you to bring him a set of plans and then does not want to see you again until he gives you the key to the front door," Dale said. "I often came up to say, 'We should have done this or that' and it bugged him. I am surprised we have not had a divorce in our relationship! But this place would not be here at this level if Keith had not invested his time and energy in the project. He saw it as leaving a legacy for his grandchildren and other children of the future."

They outlined the small town theme to several architectural firms and got varied responses.

"One firm thought we were trying to teach kids about civilization," said Mills, who had been hired in January 1989 as director for an annual salary of $24,000. "There was a trail from cave days to a futuristic city.

"The Tulsa firm hit it, with some guidance."

Jerry Beardsley of Matrix Architects Engineers Planners, Inc., in Tulsa was chosen as architect; Matrix's principal owner John Hargis was from Seminole, which seemed a perfect fit to the museum board. And the construction manager and the architect found that they worked seamlessly together throughout the construction phase.

"I received the plans and developed a budget with the funds that were available at the time, and started to work," Shaw said.

When they decided what they would like for an exhibit, Shaw would work up a budget for treasurer Ann Biddy.

"We broke the money down to this amount of funds for each exhibit," Shaw said. "For example, in Handi-Capable, we can have wheelchairs, crutches, a ramp and so on.

"We would have a Plan A, Plan B and Plan C."

The "Cadillac" plan sometimes had to be scaled back to Plan B, or even Plan C unless Melvin came up with more funding.

Once the people in Seminole found out the Morans were leading the project, everyone wanted to help.

"When I look around and see what people

gave — Larry Marker, Ronnie Allison, Jimmy Howard, Doyle Morris, R.D. Lozier, Phil Mizera, Shawnee Fire Department, Jim Goff and many others — they all did something for an exhibit," Shaw said, marveling.

"There was no way the board could do all the work that needed to be done. The dusting and cleaning the board did was good for involvement, for ownership, but the structure, the exhibits, they came about because a lot of people in Seminole contributed their time and materials at no cost. I was amazed and still am at how many stepped forward."

"I always said Seminole is a very unique city," Melvin said. "You do not find museums like this in small towns and it speaks very well for this community that we have one. The reason you do not find them in cities this size is because other towns do not have the uniqueness we have."

For their part, Melvin and Marci give a lot of credit to their construction manager.

"We needed to hire a construction manager who would take this commitment to heart," Marci said. "Keith was committed to this and he got others to commit, too. His ideas, the way he handles people, he got it done for considerably less than had we hired things done."

"Basically, we got a lot of things at cost because of Keith," Melvin said, years later. "He made only a minimal fee himself. He has been involved in everything we have built."

"We went in with hammers and crowbars," said Doyle Morris, who still was employed by the museum

18 years after that initial foray into destruction.

Shaw's team included Morris, R.D. Lozier and John Novotny.

"John had been a concrete man and I had been working in the oilfield and building houses," Morris said. "Just before hiring on at the museum, my wife, Joan and I had taken over the old Chick's hamburger joint and named it DJ's. When I got the job at the museum I would work there in the day, then go help her at the café until 10 or 11 at night."

"We all walked into the museum together on Day 1," said Lozier, who had been working as a carpenter since high school. "Day 1" was March 2, 1992. "It was a big empty building: grease pits and wash spaces, offices upstairs, remnants everywhere of what was there before."

The crew tore out walls and wires, even floors. The walls they removed changed the structure from a business with offices and storage into the open floor plan that would become a museum.

"We tore out everything except the counter out front," Morris said. "Fred Combs bought most of the ceramic tile. We pitched all the metal into a truck from Ball Pipe and Supply; it all went to Eufaula. We filled Seminole's Operation Pride truck with trash. We dug the museum's little streets with the backhoe and formed them with brick."

Lozier was the foreman for the job until one of the partial walls that would later go around the exhibits fell on him. It weighed over 1,000 pounds.

Twenty years later, his foot is still numb and

whitened scar tissue circles his ankle.

"We had four of the wall petitions done and had them pinned against the wall with an air-conditioner jack underneath," he said. "Doyle could not get the screw loose [that was holding them], so I did it. I turned around and looked up at him and his eyes were great big ...it was coming down."

The petition hit Lozier in the back and knocked him down, folding his toes underneath and crushing several bones.

"I threw him over my shoulder and hauled him out to the pickup and to the hospital," Morris said.

With Lozier injured and Shaw out of town, Morris became foreman.

"I did not tear anything up, but I didn't know what I was doing," he said.

Lozier remembers lying on his mother's couch for a week afterward, looking at those swollen purple toes.

"They looked like balloons ready to just fly off my feet at any moment," Lozier said.

After a week, he decided he could not stay still any longer.

"I could not do much, but while I was laid up, I designed Dr. Bones," Lozier said.

Dr. Bones is a skeleton on a bicycle in a glass case. When a rider pedals a matching bicycle outside the glass case, they can watch Dr. Bones making matching movements.

"I used some chains through the floor and a sprocket to make it all go around," Lozier said.

When he needed a chain guard, he created a mold and looked around for a way to melt the material into the form.

"The new kitchen had just been completed, and they had put in a professional grade convection oven," Lozier said. "We fired it up to melt down the chain guard. It worked perfectly. But that lady who put in the oven would have been really upset to know we were cooking plastic in her nice oven."

Nathylee Whitley, a member of the Science Committee, tries out Dr. Bones, a bicycling skeleton that lets children see their bones in action. *Courtesy Jacklyn Patterson Photography.*

CREATION

Usually when a museum is being built, the board will choose exhibits from a catalog. In Seminole, however, there was no money to purchase exhibits, so Shaw and a lot of other people pitched in to build them.

The architect designed the exhibit boundaries, the traffic flow, the exhibit entry ways and all the normal architectural details necessary for a museum. The committees worked with Shaw and the architect to decide how the exhibits should function.

"The ingenuity and creativity of Seminole craftsmen was unbelievable," Shaw said. "They could take a piece of paper from Bonnie Lee Grisso — she knew she wanted a Handi-Capable exhibit, but not how to do it — and turn it into a reality."

To the principals involved in building the museum, it was almost magical the way things came together.

"Keith said, 'You know, Marci, there were so many things during this construction that should not work, but for some reason, they are working,'" Marci recalled. "He said, 'There is just something about this that was meant to be.'"

Whether it was divine intervention or simple ingenuity is anybody's guess, but the museum project moved along smoothly and quickly.

During the demolition, Shaw found that the old water lines had frozen and burst during one winter after Power Transmission was closed; many leaks had to be repaired and lines replaced. Once he cut a hole in the floor and water rushed in.

"I thought I had hit a water line, but it was subsurface water," he remembered. "I wondered what in the world we were going to do. That is where the brick streets came in. They were not planned, but put in out of necessity. We cut the floors, put in a French drain and a sump pump. Then we sold bricks for $25 each. It looked like it was planned, but it was not. A lot of things here were like that."

Now, after 20 years, bricks are $50 each and a walk along the street is like a history lesson — everyone who is anyone in Oklahoma has a brick inscribed with their name, and others are dedications and memorials from all over the world.

For each exhibit, Melvin, Marci, Tommy Mills and Keith Shaw would meet with the committee chair and anyone else who wanted to and "come up with something," Shaw said.

"Usually there were more grand ideas than we could afford," Shaw added.

Teri Hooten, part of the design team, remembered her involvement clearly.

"I remember the architect came back with plans that were impractical for us," she said. "I remember different colors were up against each other, which would have been hard for us to do. We chose bright primary colors because we had children and knew those were the colors that drew their attention. We were very involved because our kids were going to play here, too."

Hooten's family grew up in the museum. She

Teri Hooten conceptualized the museum's logo, "Bringing the World to Your Child," with a string attached to a balloon as a means for children to grasp their environment. Melvin and Jasmine Moran show one rendition of her design. *Courtesy Jacklyn Patterson Photography.*

remembered announcing her pregnancy with her second child, now 20-year-old Jake, at a meeting of her committee. Later, she recalled decorating the Handi-Capable exhibit by stripping her baby to his diaper and climbing up and down a ladder holding him under one arm and a paint bucket in the other hand, then pressing his pudgy paint-covered hand to the wall for the small handprints there.

"We had to do it several times because we needed to use several colors," she said.

Hooten, a graphic designer from Ohio and owner of Teal Graphics in Seminole, designed the museum's first logo in 1988.

"After summing up her basic intuitions and some extra research on children, Teri came up with our logo," stated the museum's first newsletter.

"She envisioned the earth as a balloon floating in space with a string as the means by which children can grasp their environment. From this complex yet simplistic idea evolved the motto, 'Bringing the World to Your Child.' The impressive logo, combined with the proud motto, brought our museum concept to life."

It was used for many years before being replaced by the current logo designed by Hope Pickering of TS&H.

Throughout the museum's life, Hooten has continued to do murals and paintings as needed.

"I used my children in pictures all over the museum," she said. "You will recognize my work because of my style — sort of like cartoon images, children with big eyes. I like clean lines, happy cartoon people, smiles. I think it makes the kids feel happy."

Keith Shaw had plenty of puzzles to solve during the building phase.

"You want me to build an entryway that is 12 feet in the air, with a four-foot base and it will not tip over?" he said. "Construction-wise that is not a good thing — it is top heavy. There is so much liability and that is part of the cost of exhibits in places where kids have hands-on accessibility.

"But Phil Mizera looked at the plans, stood there awhile and figured it out."

The storefronts were painted bright colors by design team members Teri Hooten and Kathy Jett Ridgeway.

Once Shaw's team had made the tall exhibit entrances, they were hauled to an empty warehouse on Broadway where Hooten and Kathy Jett Ridgeway painted them.

"It was summertime and there was no air conditioning," Hooten remembered. "We would leave the children with babysitters and go work from 5:00 to 9:00 a.m. We would dress in our old painting clothes and put Bonnie Raitt's 'Luck of the Draw' on our little cassette player – no iPods back then! Sometimes we would listen to the radio. We had to work on the ventilation sometimes; the fumes were overwhelming. I remember getting loopy and thinking, 'We need to go outside for a bit.'"

They used oil-based paints because that was what would last longest.

"We got our paint from Sherwin Williams, they still have a card on us," Hooten said 20 years later, prior to the local Sherwin Williams store being destroyed by fire. "They had a lot of trouble finding some pink and violet we wanted. We did not use it much, but there were touches in the Bubble Room. Nowadays they would just mix it in a computer."

With the building's high ceilings, Hooten said the design team dreamed of two floors, but were told it would be too expensive. Later expansions, however, have allowed for a second story.

As the committees continued to come up with ideas for their exhibits, they would discuss it with the architect and Shaw, who, with his team, would figure out how to make it work.

"It is like when you build a church," Shaw said. "A lot of people are cautious until you start the dirt work, then when they see it is a reality and know it is going to happen, more want to participate.

"I always believed that you could call together a few Seminole people and say we have to do a job and they would sit around and put it together. It is how they are used to operating and they are not afraid of anything."

That is how Shaw saw the museum develop. He often found himself calling on people to build things they never had built before.

"A lot of people got to work outside their comfort zone and do more creative things," Marci said.

"The main thing to overcome was to convince the local plumbers, electricians, carpenters and others that they could build an exhibit," Shaw said. "Once that was accomplished, they got behind the project with enthusiasm."

An example was the aquarium. The budget was $144,000.

"You cannot buy the glass for that, much less build a cave and waterfalls, put in a filtration system," Shaw said. "So I contacted Tom Cole Plumbing, one of the best plumbers around here, and Joe Robinson of Robinson Stone. Tom, his son Wade, Joe and I sat down and started brainstorming. We needed rock in the water inside the aquarium, a cave, trees and other things that would make the exhibit look natural.

"We knew we could not buy an artificial exhibit tree; at the time, they were $10,000 each."

Tom and Wade Cole went to the John G. Shedd Aquarium in Chicago, researched and decided they could build an aquarium.

"Once their interest was piqued, they wanted to be a part of the Children's Museum," Shaw said. "And the aquarium has functioned successfully for these many years."

Most museum exhibits are designed and built off-site, then installed, which makes them much more expensive. The way the Seminole entrepreneurs kept the project local made for great "ownership" of the project and saved immeasurable expense, according to Shaw.

Because he himself had worked as a teacher and school administrator for 10 years, Shaw had some knowledge of children and how they learn and interact.

"When I walk into a museum, now, I look around and think, 'There is no telling what this cost,'" Shaw said. "I think 'We could do this for a fraction of the cost and it will look almost as good.' We were able to put this museum together through people contributing what they had — even if it was a tractor tire."

In the Bubble Room, "we did not spend much at all," Shaw said. "We said, 'This is the money we have; here is what we can do with it.' And the exhibit is still functioning 20 years later."

R.D. Lozier vividly remembers putting together

the Bubble Room, which he still thinks of as the "coolest" part of the museum.

"Tommy and Melvin had been somewhere and seen such an apparatus," Lozier said. "Of course neither of them could drive a nail. I automatically pictured what they were talking about and decided to see what I could do."

He gathered up "a lot of junk from around the museum," including an aluminum pan, which he drilled with holes.

"I used PVC for the soap screen and filled it with glycerin and water, just like those little bottles of bubbles you buy at the store," Lozier said.

"I took it to Tommy's office and set it on his desk. I raised the ring and it made a perfect bubble.

"Tommy was amazed," Lozier said, still smiling about it 20 years later, "He said, 'There is only one thing...it needs to be bigger.'

"I said, 'Tommy, it is just a prototype.'"

Lozier said he found the plumbing supplies he needed from a contractor in Georgia. He bought a sheet of galvanized metal from Fred Combs, who had a metal bender.

"Then I thought of a tractor tire to hold the water and glycerin," he said.

"It took me two days to cut it in two and I do not know how many saw blades I broke. There was steel wire in the tire."

He formed a "hula hoop" from PVC.

"It worked," Lozier. said. "Everybody loves it

The late Wayman Tisdale, basketball and jazz star, enjoyed the Bubble Room during a visit to the Children's Museum.

and there have been plenty of celebrities to try it out."

Lozier set up the sandpit outside that holds the slide and swings. He had a pry bar he used to chip holes for the posts. The ground then was covered in black mesh to keep out weeds, which was next covered in rock.

"Tony [Lenora] laid my pry bar down and it got covered with rocks," Lozier said. "I asked, 'Where is my pry bar?' Tony could not remember exactly where he had put it.

"Earl Bowen gave me that pry bar and I did not want to lose it."

Doyle Morris found someone with a metal detector and dug up the bar.

As exhibits were being decided, Melvin and Jasmine remembered a longtime artist acquaintance who might help with certain projects. They called Marilyn and Richard Fulton, former Seminole residents now living in Enid, and met them in Oklahoma City for dinner to ask for their help.

The couples had met while the Fultons lived in Seminole during the 1950s, 1960s and early 1970s. A Tulsa High School graduate, Marilyn Fulton said she cannot remember a time when she did not draw, although the only formal training she ever had was a correspondence course after her four children were born. The family moved to Seminole, when husband Dick was transferred by Humble Oil. In Seminole Marilyn gave art classes and the Morans' children attended.

Marilyn Fulton painted a bus mural high on the museum's south wall using portraits of several of the museum builders and their family members.

These days the Fultons live in Enid. A colorful character, Fulton always dresses herself and her husband in purple. Their house is purple and they have a purple car.

Marilyn, at 80, talks about the time not all that long ago when she went rappelling and sifts through photos and clippings on every desk, table, sofa, chair and footstool of her house looking for the video of her recent sky-diving episode.

In 1978, Marilyn had been hired to paint a mural of historic Seminole scenes on a brick wall facing the parking lot of BancFirst, where Melvin is on the Board of Directors. After moving to Enid, she became well known for murals in city parks and schools all over town.

Marilyn painted the bus mural which is high on the south wall overlooking the museum's main floor. The bus is filled with the children and grandchildren of workers and contributors. For the three months it took to paint the mural, she traveled to Seminole, staying with Barbara and Kenneth Mendenhall, and sometimes with the Morans.

"I would try to go in as early as possible and work as many hours on it as I could," she said.

During the time Marilyn was working on scaffolding high above the museum's concrete floor, she said she suffered from sleep apnea.

"I was painting the word 'Oklahoma' on the school bus and went to sleep," she recalled. "For some reason I painted an 'S.' We got it fixed but for awhile, it read 'Soklahoma.'"

When she could not reach the highest corner of the mural from her scaffolding, a forklift was brought in to lift her up.

Lozier's accident is documented as part of the museum's history in the bus mural. He is pictured as the bus driver, his little crutches visible in the glass of the bus' door. Morris' son Wayland, Keith's twin grandchildren, accountant Ann Biddy's daughter, Lauren, all are in the mural, as is Melvin himself and three of his grandchildren.

"We would just give her a picture and she would paint them in," Morris said.

"I was the only person that she painted live," Lozier said. "I actually climbed up on the scaffolding to let her paint me."

The mural's original design included balloons, but they later were cut.

Working alone in the museum, Marilyn took tours of the exhibits, even sliding down the fire pole once.

"When we were finished, Melvin asked what would be the full price for the mural and I wrestled with that question," she said. "Finally I told him how much it would have cost and he put on the plaque that we donated that much."

CREATION

Administration

administration (ad-min-uh-strey-shuhn), n.
the management of any office, business,
or organization; direction

BEHIND THE SCENES

As the museum took shape, the fundraisers seemed to have an almost profound ability to find money.

"By then we had a visual product to sell," Marci said. "You have to prove yourself before you can go on fundraising."

More than 90 percent of the presentations seeking grants and donations were made by Melvin and Marci.

"We were successful, we believe, because of our passion for the museum," Melvin said. "Our passion obviously comes through when we seek help."

"Ideas are like highly contagious organisms; they are powerful and spread like wildfire," said Dr. Carmen Notaro, who was hired by the museum and Seminole State College, through the efforts of Jim Cook, President Emeritus of SSC and museum board member, in 1995 to write grants for both entities.

He established the Office of Development at the Jasmine Moran Children's Museum.

"The museum concept came to fruition because of the quiet persistence of the Morans," Notaro said. "They never gave up on their plan to establish a museum...their tenacity to get other people excited about the idea and to get involved was brilliantly infectious."

Notaro saw the project as "mutual inspiration."

"I have observed Jasmine quietly," he said. "She is just as much of a powerhouse as her husband, Melvin."

He first met the Morans in 1991 at St. Gregory's College in Shawnee.

"I was impressed with their humanness and warmth," he said. "Melvin did the formal presentation and Jasmine did her fundraising work behind the scenes with an unassuming eloquence."

Jasmine first introduced Notaro to the museum's brick pathway program and was "convincing and powerful," he said.

"Jasmine and Melvin believe so much in the principal of giving," he said. "As a couple, they are active in many charitable causes and civic organizations across Oklahoma. So it was only right that when they had a cause, influential people, who were involved as members of other community organizations, rallied to help them with the idea of supporting a children's museum."

Despite Melvin's self-deprecating assertion that he knew nothing about fundraising, Notaro, a professional fundraiser, found him to be "accomplished" and prone to perseverance.

"Melvin is also a gifted wordsmith," Notaro said. "When you put Melvin's tenacity as a fundraiser and the gift of good writing together, it is a powerful combination that succeeds in reaping donations initially and over the long haul."

Notaro saw from the Morans that effective fundraising is not just gift-giving; it is about being a good citizen or corporation involved in a good cause, then watching the excitement escalate.

"Melvin is a master at the responsible approach," Notaro said. "The twinkle in Jasmine's eyes seal the deal."

He commended their idea to get many of the people they knew involved by adding them to the board.

"Donations themselves are not what the history of Jasmine Moran Children's Museum is about," Notaro said. "But without essential monetary support and without Melvin and Jasmine's obvious talents in this important area, the idea of a children's museum would not have succeeded, pure and simple."

Notaro believes that part of the fundraising process is showing respect for the possible donor following a first encounter, on the occasion of a meeting, or the celebration of a commitment promised and even on the occasion of no gift.

"Melvin is a master in the area of personal contact," Notaro said.

He also found that he and Melvin worked well together.

"As [Seminole State College] President Cook remarked several times, we both were research-oriented and wanted the work done yesterday," Notaro said.

While the construction and fundraising continued, even a huge garage sale in 1991 helped raise money for the project, the museum board also kept busy.

"Melvin made our job easy," said Dr. Jim Cook, who served on the executive board almost from the beginning, and as vice-chair for awhile. "We did not have to sit around thinking about things to try; he already had the ideas.

"Now if my wife has an idea, I would say, 'well, maybe.' But if Melvin Moran has an idea, he is determined to make it happen. If he makes a decision that he is going to be actively involved, he will achieve the goal, whatever it is. And he was so excited about this."

Cook said the board usually just provided discussion on the pros and cons of Melvin's ideas.

"We discussed the practical things," he said. "How would we get so much money? What to charge for admission, where to park the buses, how many tables do we need for the lunch area, should there be a café or not?

"There were so many details of operation. How many do we hire, how much will they be paid, how to stock and oversee inventory in the gift shop.

"We were open to the public, so we had to be aware of our liability. We had to paint these curbs where the kids are dropped off, we need to make this one-way. There were logistical problems. We needed someone to tell visitors the rules before they went in. How many kids per adult should we recommend, where will they put trash, who will paint the parking lot, do we need to take bids? There is a roof leak over here."

To him, it seemed remarkable that the museum went from an idea to a first-rate concern so quickly.

"Keith Shaw and Tommy Mills had their hands full trying to keep up with Melvin's ideas," Cook said. "It was a foreign environment for almost all of us involved. Few had experience in this field and there was no close model. It is amazing that things stayed organized enough to get off the ground. I remember Tommy telling us how he did it: 'We will eat this elephant one bite at a time.'"

Mills explained the motto.

"I heard a story about a tribe in Africa where it was a rite of passage for boys to go with hunters to kill an elephant," he said. "After killing the elephant, a little boy asked what they were going to do with it. He was told, 'We are going to eat it.'"

The child asked how and his grandfather replied, "One bite at a time, my son, one bite at a time."

"Sometimes things would loom so large we would get frustrated," Mills said. It made things easier for everyone to remember his adage, "One bite at a time."

All those involved early on spent many hours on the project.

"I remember thinking, 'Well, it is only one night a month,'" Cook said, laughing. "At least that is what they said."

"Melvin," Cook added, "put in 90 percent of the work."

"He presented the board with the problem and said, 'Here is what I think; what do you think?' We would discuss it and then we would vote on it," he said.

Did the board ever disagree with Melvin's ideas?

"I would say it was very rare," Cook said. "I am usually not hesitant about saying, 'Are you sure? Can we check on this?' I am a 'worst case scenario' kind of guy, not to be negative, but to make sure we have thought about all the implications. If we figure out what is the worst thing that can happen and plan for it, we can say, 'We thought of that and have it covered.'"

One of Cook's biggest contributions was the operations manual.

"That is my area of expertise because I had written the first comprehensive operations manual at Seminole State," he said. "I started on it in 1987 and modeled it after the State Regents' format.

"I like rules, guidelines. If you have to fire someone, you have to have some basic accounting."

The board looked at financial reports and

debated what would happen if the next donation did not come in.

"Yes, the budget was that close until we got the word out," Cook said. "How do you get teachers and superintendents from Ardmore to come up if you do not know someone there to promote it? Maybe you will give incentives. I think one of the first things we did was presenting a free day to a school district to get the word-of-mouth going."

Marilyn Moran-Townsend's video company prepared a new promotional video, which the museum staff sent to school teachers. It shows a school bus, driven by former Seminole Chamber of Commerce Director Bob Jones, full of children pulling up to the museum. Their teacher is played by Marci. The children interact with the exhibits and talk about what they want to be when they grow up. Jones and Marci say the museum is fun for adults as well as children and also play in "fast time." It becomes hilarious when the bus driver ties the teacher to the tracks when the train is coming.

They also prepared an orientation video, giving the adults accompanying those groups of children a list of rules regarding the "dos" and "don'ts" of the museum.

The Jasmine Moran Children's Museum was a chance to start something new, creative and challenging and that is the type of people who joined the project. Despite the economic downturn that the city had been facing, the period of museum-building was a golden one for Seminole.

"In Seminole, if there is a legitimate need for something, you can find folks to volunteer," Cook said. "Maybe they would be political opponents, or not go to the same church, or be simpatico on other things, but they will work well together for something for their town. Is that attitude prevalent everywhere? I do not think so."

Melvin's long-held reputation as a peacemaker may have contributed to the "get along" mindset in Seminole. For many years, whenever there have been rifts between groups, from the Chamber of Commerce, to the schools, to the city officials, Melvin has often become personally involved to soothe hurt feelings and smooth ruffled feathers.

The attitude of pitching in to make something work can be found not only in the way the museum was built, but also how it was staffed. The board decided that most of the staffing could be volunteers.

According to the first-ever Children's Museum newsletter, published in the fall of 1990, a reception was held July 12, 1990, at the emerging museum to introduce the project to the local citizenry. More than 150 attended and 30 people were signed up to work as volunteers. A second reception was held on August 27, 1990, which broadened the exposure of the museum to visitors from across the state. Many of the advisory board members, who had loaned their name and support to the museum, were able to see the project for the first time. They actually saw children playing with a few early exhibits: an electronic "step-on" keyboard, the magnet table and domino display. A highlight of the evening was the introduction of Kermie Gee, the robot financed by Kerr-McGee Corporation's donation.

At one point, executive director Tommy Mills, Melvin, Marci and board member Liz Robertson sat in the museum café with a phone book in front of each. They went through every name in the phone book, and in almost every case, one of the organizers knew someone in that household. They wrote down the names of those who might make good volunteers, then called or sent them letters.

"It was not long before we decided we also needed teenaged volunteers," Melvin said. "We went to schools and asked teens to volunteer."

They found that the teens who were active socially or in extracurricular activities did not have time to volunteer.

"Our volunteers came mostly from teenagers who did not participate in activities, and many were introverts," Melvin said. "Some came from families where children were told, 'If you see a police officer, run.'"

The first volunteer coordinator was Seminole Police Chief Steve Williams.

"Steve transformed our teenaged volunteers," Melvin said. "He taught them that police officers were good people who could help them."

Williams established a dress code and a courtesy code and, before long, being a volunteer at the Children's Museum was the "cool thing" to do

ADMINISTRATION

Volunteering at the Children's Museum gave area teens camaraderie and taught them good work ethics.
Photo Courtesy Jacklyn Patterson Photographer.

in Seminole.

"Our youth docent program was a 'first job' for our youth," Marci said. "They had responsibilities much like our paid adult staff.

"My belief was that our youth program provided a special place for some who might otherwise not feel acceptance in other settings. Our staff did a great job of mentoring to many of the youths while teaching them those soft skills needed in today's work place. Building self-confidence and self-esteem were also critical components to our youth program."

Volunteers had personal time cards on which they clocked in and out. They were recognized for their hours of service at an annual Thanksgiving dinner held at Seminole State College, hosted by the Morans. Other perks included parties and outings, such as trips to Six Flags.

The museum later lowered the age for volunteering, so kids as young as 10 could participate. Parents often told Melvin or Marci that they could not wait for their children to be old enough to volunteer.

Unfortunately, the youth volunteer program became labor-intensive for the staff, and the program was dropped in 2011.

Once while visiting the only children's museum in England, Jasmine and Melvin found that the smaller museum employed 100 people.

"In Seminole, our paid staff varies from 12 to 14 and the majority of the staff works part-time," Melvin

When the museum opened, Doyle Morris was hired to care for the museum on a daily basis. He often brought his grandsons, Ross and Justin Parker, to help him.

said. "Without our volunteers, the Children's Museum in Seminole could not financially exist; so we are grateful to our volunteers."

During his time of constructing the museum, Doyle Morris once thought, "This would be a good place for a maintenance man."

"I never dreamed it would be me," he said. "I think if R.D. had not gotten hurt, he would have gotten the permanent job as head of maintenance, but they offered it to me."

"I realized that the museum is only as good as the maintenance," said Jasmine. As she has visited museums, she said she was unhappy to see exhibits not working properly or in poor repair. She did not want that for this museum.

"We knew we needed a quality person to take care of this," she said. "With Doyle, we have never had anything not working for more than a day. He is a wonderful person."

Morris had visited the building once while it was still the old Power Transmission building.

"I had to take some hydraulic hoses to be fixed," he recalled. "That back door was the one I used and, years later, it ended up being the door to my office."

Morris was holding the front door open when the museum opened on January 23, 1993, three years later than was originally planned, but beating the national average by eight months.

Imagination

IMAGIN

imagination (ih-maj-uh-ney-shuhn), n.
the product of imagining; a conception or mental
creation, the faculty of imagining

As God's indiscernible clock ticked down toward the museum's opening, the former oilfield business was filled with cool, colorful exhibits. Walls were covered in murals painted by local and once-local artists like Marilyn Fulton, April Jones and Teri Hooten. The Children's Theater was designed to look like the Royal Drury Lane Theater where Jasmine Moran performed in the musical *South Pacific*. A gift shop offered trinkets and nicer gifts and a small restaurant was built to the specifications of Seminole's Lunch 'n' Such owner Helen Adams.

"Vivian Mills volunteered to set up and organize the gift shop," said accountant Ann Biddy. "She is very talented. Sometimes around noontime I would come down and help out because I knew it would be chaotic in there. For awhile, we only let five kids come in a time."

The long brick hallway from the foyer to the exhibit hall was lined on one side with the names

Jeanne Frame, right, was one of the first managers of the museum's gift shop, which was set up and organized by executive director Tommy Mills' talented wife Vivian. *Courtesy C.J. Vigil.*

of individuals, corporations and foundations whose contributions made the museum possible, and on the other side by plaques with the museum's motto and mission statement.

At the end of the hall hung a huge painting of children of several races against a blue-sky background, depicting friendship, diversity and tolerance. Well-known Native American painter Kelly Haney collaborated with his son for the work. The painting used many Oklahoma symbols like the scissor-tailed flycatcher, the Indian paintbrush and the eagle.

Doyle Morris, who had worked on the construction phase and later was hired as head of maintenance for the museum, remembered picking up the twelve-foot by six-foot painting from Kelly Haney's home studio.

"Tommy sent me out to Kelly's house in my pickup," Morris said. "The painting was so big it fit the bed of my pickup perfectly. I tied it down with bungee cords.

"Kelly said that if it did not fit we could peel back the canvas and saw it off with a table saw. I thought, 'Sure we will.' It was only later that I found it was worth $50,000."

Rounding the corner into the main exhibit area was the dollhouse built by Marilyn and Dick Fulton. They had been so excited when asked to work on the dollhouse and a diorama to surround a donated electric train valued at $10,000.

"We bought a kit for the house, but of course

we had to make it bigger," Marilyn said of the dollhouse. The end result was about four feet by six feet, a warm yellow-sided, three-story manor.

They created an office as much like Melvin's as possible, with a miniature Melvin at a miniature desk. A bottle cap served as a tin for an apple pie in the kitchen. A crocheted cloth covered the tiny dining table. Eggs and other foods fashioned from dough filled the small refrigerator. They even made holiday decorations to be stored in the little house's attic. Dick built a fence around the house and Marilyn created paper flowers for the yard.

The Fultons made the project into a kind of treasure hunt, haunting antique and junk shops, as well as craft stores. They found things by divine chance and used their apparently limitless imagination to make things out of nothing.

"One thing led into the next so easily," Marilyn Fulton said, echoing a theme heard throughout the building process.

There was no budget for the dollhouse. They would just give their receipts to Melvin and they were paid.

"He never questioned them and that encouraged us to be even more honest, I think," she said. "I could never steal, but especially from such an honest man. Trust means a lot."

Marilyn said she felt she could ask Melvin for anything.

"He would say, 'Do you think it is a good idea? Okay, then, let's do it,'" she said.

Next the couple built a small train diorama of the state of Oklahoma, with many figures and buildings from the Seminole area. They worked on it at home and it filled their garage. They had to crawl underneath to work on the back.

"It had to fit in the allotted space at the museum, so it was a smaller scale than the normal HO scale," she said. For the same reason, tight turns were necessary, making some parts of the project even more difficult. A little carnival and a waterfall completed the scene.

After the train was finished, Marilyn felt it looked too stark with the white wall behind, so she painted a scene on the wall as backdrop.

Doyle Morris' favorite part of the museum was

Marilyn and Dick Fulton completed a dollhouse for the museum that included Melvin Moran's office and a tiny Melvin Moran.

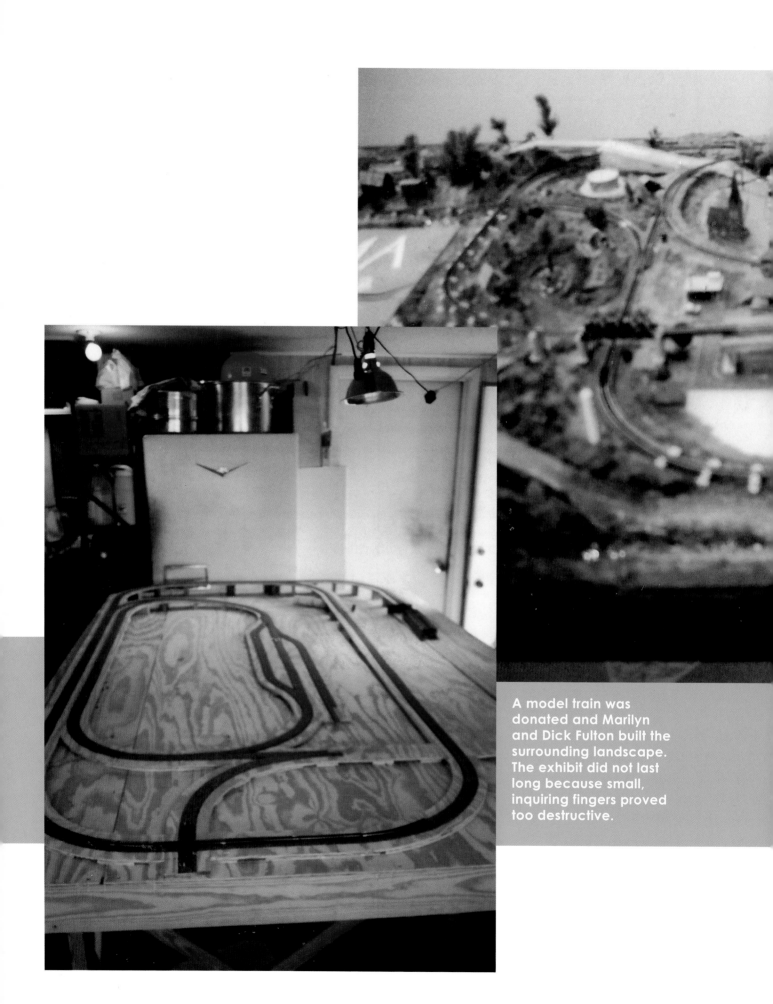

A model train was donated and Marilyn and Dick Fulton built the surrounding landscape. The exhibit did not last long because small, inquiring fingers proved too destructive.

the aquarium, which he took over when he was hired as head of maintenance. The aquarium's frame came from Tyler, Texas, he recalled.

The aquarium began with the help of Tom and Wade Cole of Cole Plumbing, and Joe Robinson of Robinson Stone. The Coles, father and son, took a trip to the Shedd Aquarium in Chicago, to get tips on putting in the aquarium.

"That rock on the back wall is an exact cast of that rocky cliff that used to be on the right side going out on West Strother toward Pleasant Grove," said Morris, referring to Joe Robinson's stone work. "The cliff is not there any more."

Wade Cole was primarily in charge of putting in the aquarium, but was seriously injured in a car wreck, working inside the aquarium at times in a neck brace, before leaving the project.

"The kids thought he was part of the exhibit and would wave to him," Morris said, laughing.

When Cole left the project, Morris used his notes and took over the aquarium.

"I had fished all my life," Morris said.

First he went around picking up stumps from the North Canadian and Little River — they are still there in the aquarium.

"I found one big rock over on Twin Oak Road and was trying to get it into my pickup," Morris said. "I was wallering that rock all over the road when Crazy Jack Fowler and Tommy Eads happened upon me. They had a truck with a gin pole and helped me get it loaded."

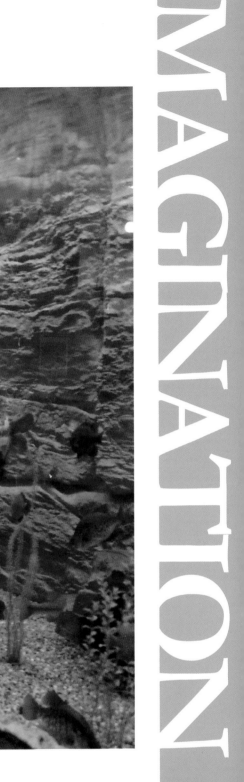

Doyle Morris took over the operation of the aquarium after Wade Cole was injured in a car accident. The aquarium became Morris' favorite part of the museum. *Courtesy Jacklyn Patterson Photography.*

When the exhibit needed a tree, Morris found one over on Ideal Street. He came up with the old tire for the pollution part of the aquarium exhibit.

Local artist Teri Hooten remembered doing the paintings by the aquarium.

"In the 'polluted' area, I just painted what I had had for lunch that day – there is an apple core, a Mountain Dew can and a Snickers wrapper," she said.

R.D. Lozier remembered spending the night on the Deep Fork River near IXL, Oklahoma, to catch the first fish for the aquarium.

"We woke up in the morning and our nets were all tied up," he said. "We had caught a 10-pound flathead. We put him in the aquarium and he dove straight under that rock at the east end and that became his spot. He grew from this big [holding his hands about two feet apart] to this big [about four feet]. Doyle said he ate everything he put in there: perch, crappie."

Lozier also remembered adding the rooted stumps to the aquarium.

"One of them started floating up and Doyle said he would just get in there and swim down to put some rocks on it," Lozier said.

"He got in and tried to swim to the bottom, but his pants kept filling with air and that kept his backside up on top of the water. We laughed and laughed. He kept trying to swim down, but he could not get there. Finally he had to come up for air. I think he eventually used a long pole to move some rocks over it."

Many of the other fish Morris caught made their way into the 13,500-gallon aquarium. Others were contributed by museum supporters who were surprised and delighted to see their fish when they visited.

Morris and his friends still laugh about the turtle he once saved by mouth-to-mouth resuscitation. "He is still living out in that pond in back," Morris laughed. "His name was Tripod; Buzz Gillespie still always asks me about Tripod when he sees me."

"Many of the fish died when they were put into the new tank," Morris remembered.

"I tried to figure it all out," he said. "I saved every fish and turtle that ever died in the freezer until we finally had to throw them all out when it was full. I did post mortems on them to find out what went wrong. I could tell if a fish was sick or not."

He believed the problem was the fiberglass and glue, and the fact that the fish were placed directly in the water without quarantining them to get used to the water.

"The fire department had brought in water from Sportsmans Lake," Morris said. "I drained the tank and used clean city water. Doe McRay built a filter. A guy from the hatcheries over at Holdenville said to put salt in the water to kill disease. I tried it and it worked."

He remembered how he and co-worker Tony Lenora worried over the fish. The night he filled the tank he left the water on and went home.

"I figured it would take all night," he said. "Next morning, Tony came in and sprayed a little water on the floor and the door. When I came in and saw that, I went flying to the aquarium – I was sure it had overflowed. Tony was standing over there laughing at me."

"There was a flood one time, though. The first winter, the fire sprinklers were a little close to the heater," Morris said.

"Those little glasses in the sprinkler system got hot and it went off," he recalled. "We sucked water out of the brick streets for days." The company that put in the sprinkler system came back and put in higher temperature glass for the sprinklers.

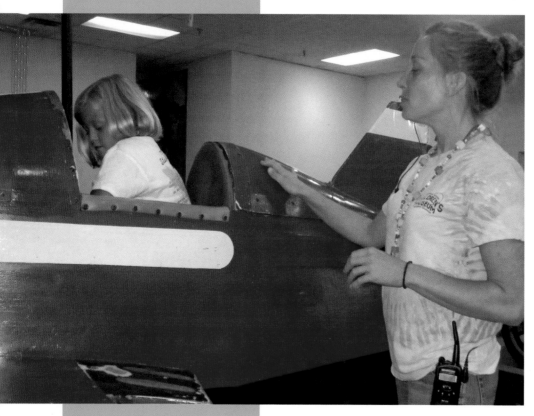

Staff member Jennifer Cheatham Mattson supervises visitor Marin Adams, seven, in the flight simulator built by Tulsa Technology Center. Before the museum opened, construction worker R.D. Lozier was the only one small enough to get into the plane for the test drive. *Courtesy Karen Anson.*

KidTown Park, where the aquarium was located, also was where one could find the 1921 Model T, the Convair aircraft and the flight simulator. Hand-painted murals depicted an Oklahoma landscape.

The old Convair cockpit, built to jut out of the west wall of the museum, is believed to have flown in the Berlin airlift. Although there is no documentation, museum organizers were told it was one of the U.S.

Air Force planes that flew over 200,000 missions in 1948-1949, bringing 4,700 tons of daily necessities such as fuel and food to West Berlin during the blockade by the Soviet Union.

The museum acquired the plane through the intervention of then State Representative Danny Williams. Tulsa Technology Center had refurbished it and they also made the cockpit fit into the museum wall.

"We could not find a place for it," said accountant Ann Biddy. "We thought of putting it in the parking lot, but there was no way the cars could get around it. It was my idea to put it in the wall. The kids really like it."

Dale Donaho convinced the FAA to do a recording for the cockpit which simulated a flight from Seminole to Oklahoma City, "Something most kids would never really know about," Donaho said.

Another aero-space exhibit was the flight simulator, a small Red Baron-esque plane on which children could ride up and down, was also an idea from Marci's husband.

"I belong to an aerobatic club that helped put on the Aerospace America Air Show in Oklahoma City," Donaho said. "I had seen a simulator and thought that would be a unique thing for kids. I suggested the idea and then we got Tulsa Technology Center to actually build it."

When it was time to test drive the plane, only the smallest of the museum workers, R.D. Lozier, could fit inside for the maiden voyage.

There were about 40 model planes donated

by Jim and Kevin Danner of Norman. Keith Shaw built the display for the models, which had the airplanes mounted with a motor propelling them inside a glass case.

Visitors could leave the part of the museum called KidTown Park through the cave next to the aquarium and re-enter the main gallery of KidTown.

When First National Bank closed, the beautiful black marble from the Seminole bank became available to the museum. It was used in six triangular memorials placed in the floor at intersections throughout the museum, commemorating the name of someone instrumental in the building of the museum. The first was inscribed in gold to the Morans. The streets were given real street signs and named for the major contributors to the museum.

During the creation phase, Jasmine and Melvin took their children and grandchildren to Disneyworld in Orlando, Florida. They visited Epcot Center and were impressed with an exhibit which uses video to impose children's images onto a screen, allowing them to interact with their on-screen image.

Their daughter, Marilyn Moran-Townsend, CEO of Custom Video Communications in Fort Wayne, Indiana, said she could create the exhibit and improve on it so a video could be made of the children playing with their on-screen images.

The exhibit, named Video Magic at the Children's Museum, provided the video for a nominal fee for the children to take home. Later the video was upgraded to a DVD.

"Visitors love the magic of standing in front of a green wall and seeing themselves appear inside the action that is in the museum – the aquarium, inside a bubble, on the puppet stage, flying through the museum..." Moran-Townsend said.

Next door was the television studio where children sat at a desk in front of five clocks showing different time zones and a map of the world, reminiscent of the old 1950's television news sets. A camera recorded their "newscasts." And a sound and light control box provided all the buttons and switches a child could ever want to press, flip and spin.

The television studio was sponsored by McDonald's. Instrumental in getting funding was Kathy Thorley from Ada, who, with her husband, Rick, own several McDonald's restaurants, including the one in Seminole.

A puppet theater encouraged children to be someone or something else. In the Infinity Mirror Room, kids could look at themselves in various distorted mirrors, gyrating to see themselves taller, shorter, fatter and thinner. Thelma Arnold, a local artist and Melvin's secretary, and her daughter, Heather Dillon, painted the figures in the Mirror Room, as well as those in the Shadow room.

"I designed and built all those mirrors of Plexiglas, with curvatures to distort the images," R.D. Lozier recalled. "How did I learn to do that? I just used my imagination."

In the Shadow Room, children stood against a special material that absorbs light when a strobe flashed. The children moved away from the wall to look at their shadows as they began to fade from the surface. The interesting shapes caused by out flung arms or legs never fail to amaze visitors.

The museum that inspired the Seminole residents had a judge's bench, but they chose to improve on the courthouse setting with an entire courtroom scaled to kid-size. Children could imagine

Melissa Bevelhymer is "interrogated" and "judged" during a 1990's museum visit. *Courtesy Jacklyn Patterson Photography.*

what it was like to be a judge, a witness, a juror or an attorney. The jury box was placed next to a television, where kids, serving as jurors, pushed a button to see one of six situation videos dealing with racial, religious or gender discrimination, lying, cheating or other dilemmas. The drama was acted out by children and the visitor made choices with the push of a red or green button. Their vote would continue the drama until the judge, former Oklahoma District 22 Judge Gordon Melson, who also served on the museum's Advisory board, came on screen to advise the jury if they had made the right decision.

"All the dramas were created to teach children ethics," Melvin said. The idea for the courtroom video came from his daughter, Marilyn Moran-Townsend; she and her company wrote the scripts and created the videos.

"We got pews from an old courthouse in western Oklahoma," Keith Shaw said. "At the time, that was all we could afford."

But the old benches were beautifully refinished, stained and lacquered, along with the judge's bench and jury box. The three branches of government were depicted in a tree mural behind the judge, along with the Great Seal of Oklahoma. The acting judge would sit on his/her bench in pretend robes and bang a gavel.

"It was Gordon's idea to contact [Oklahoma City attorney] Lana Tyree for the courthouse exhibit," said Melvin. "She donated $5,000."

The Handi-Capable exhibit teaches normal children what it is like to have physical limitations. They use crutches, walker or wheelchair to travel on uneven surfaces like grass, stone and brick, or try to drink from a water fountain. They can enter a soundproof room to experience the quiet world of the hearing impaired, or use a brailler to learn about the world of the visually impaired.

"Early on, Marci told me of her idea of a Handi-Capable exhibit," Melvin said. "During our creation stage, I was attending an oil convention in Boston and I visited the Boston Children's Museum, which I believe is the oldest children's museum in America."

There Melvin saw an exhibit almost exactly like Marci had wanted.

"When Bonnie Lee Grisso and her team were assigned the Handi-Capable exhibit, we wanted to convey to our guests that just because people may have some kind of physical limitation, they are not handicapped, but Handi-Capable," Marci explained. "I was adamant that the exhibit should be named Handi-Capable and everyone agreed. My feeling was that when our guests, particularly our younger ones, experience what it is like to be in a wheelchair, walker, crutches, or using a brailler, perhaps an awareness would develop to be more sensitive to the needs of those with some kind of physical limitation. Maybe they would be more inclined to open a door or assist in some helpful way."

The Handi-Capable exhibit in Boston was

Children learn what it is like to live with handicaps in the Handi-Capable exhibit. *Courtesy Jacklyn Patterson Photography.*

sponsored by the Ronald McDonald House Charities, so Melvin hoped they might sponsor such an exhibit in Seminole.

"I knew that a request from someone in Seminole, Oklahoma, to McDonald's would not get much attention," Melvin said. "So I thought, 'Who do I know who is connected to McDonald's?' My first response was, 'No one.'"

Then he remembered a college fraternity brother going to work for McDonald's after college many years before. He was a year behind Melvin in school and they had not been in contact for 35 years.

"I had no idea where he was living or if he still had any connection to McDonald's," Melvin said. "His name was Irv Klein and he was originally from Coffeyville, Kansas."

Melvin contacted several former fraternity brothers and, after about eight contacts, found someone who knew that Irv Klein was now living in New York.

"I called Irv and the first 30 minutes of our conversation was spent bringing each other up on our lives and our families," Melvin remembered.

He learned that Klein did not work for McDonald's, but owned five of the restaurants.

"I asked Irv if there was some way he could put us in touch with Ronald McDonald House Charities," Melvin said.

In the way that good fortune happens to Melvin and the museum, Klein not only knew someone, but was himself serving on the board of Ronald McDonald House Charities, located near Chicago.

"I am not convinced that this was a coincidence," Melvin said. "I believe that someone up there was continuing to help us."

Melvin told Klein about the Children's Museum and asked if he thought Ronald McDonald House Charities might assist with funding for the Handi-Capable exhibit. Klein said he would put in a good word on one condition: that Melvin and Jasmine join him and his wife Mina for a week of vacation.

"Of course, I immediately agreed," Melvin said. "The four of us had a terrific time together and we vacationed with Irv and Mina for one week for the next 10 years."

They were joined by another fraternity brother, Norman Saunders, and his wife, Gloria, who also lived in New York.

"With the support of Irv, the national Ronald McDonald House Charities funded our Handi-Capable exhibit," Melvin said. "Over the next few years, they also funded two other major exhibits."

Creativity Central was the arts and crafts area funded by various art groups. Children could express themselves through painting, weaving, sculpting and drawing to stimulate artistic expression. Supplies filled white cabinets and paintings dried in wire racks. Red chairs and purple tables brightened the area. The nature of Creativity Central required that a staff person or volunteer almost always be on hand to

Everyone is a budding artist at heart and Creativity Central fosters those dreams. *Courtesy Jacklyn Patterson Photography.*

distribute supplies. Although cleanup would be a labor-intensive task, the area would soon become not only popular with the kids but with the volunteers and staff as well.

Children love to play school, so a child-sized classroom gave them a place to have fun while learning. They could role play and use computers with a variety of educational programs. Rows of desks and a teacher's desk were joined by the customary blackboard and alphabet posters.

The Bubble Factory used simple tools to let visitors make bubbles of various sizes and shapes. The highlight there was a platform on which the visitor could pull a cord to draw up a hoop from inside a tractor tire full of bubble solution, encasing themselves in their own bubble. Wands of varying shapes and sizes, a bubble machine and a soap screen made exploration fun. Floors there were covered with rubber mats to keep children from sliding down. The rubber drained away water and the bubble solution. Teri Hooten painted the mural.

Museum founder Melvin Moran is in the museum every day, walking through the galleries, playing with the children and checking with the director. He often is found teaching a young visitor how to use one of the bubble makers in the Bubble Factory.

Larry Marker renovated the old 1936 fire truck donated by the City of Seminole. Who knows how many firefighters the city has reaped from that donation. *Courtesy Jacklyn Patterson Photography.*

The Kid Town Fire Station included equipment and kid-sized fire gear for children to don, as well as a fire pole to slide down; the pole was donated by the Shawnee Fire Department. The entry was a Dalmatian spot-painted archway.

Construction Manager Keith Shaw said Wewoka resident Larry Marker volunteered to redo the old 1936 fire truck. It had been donated by the City of Seminole.

"He drove it up one day and it was a powder puff," Shaw said. "We did not pay him to do it. But these people are not used to getting credit. They did

Homeland sponsors a miniature grocery store, where children can shop, scan and package pretend food to their heart's delight. *Courtesy Jacklyn Patterson Photography.*

not do it for that reason. They are not used to being on boards. They did it because the museum was a good idea and they wanted to participate."

Nearly every children's museum that the JMCM organizers visited had a grocery store. They contacted Homeland, which agreed to sponsor the store. Homeland built the museum's miniature store and agreed to keep it stocked with pretend groceries.

Visitors chose to be managers, checkers, stockers or shoppers in a miniature supermarket, with a cart, shelves and cash register. At the end, they were encouraged to put away their groceries. One young man, who is now a Homeland corporate employee, remembered his time as a youngster playing in the museum and has now taken personal pride to keep the exhibit fresh with new items.

A hospital setting encouraged children to investigate the world of medicine with the use of microscopes, computers and equipment. They learned about the human body and its functions. A real ambulance, built into the east wall of the museum, gave them an abundance of buttons to push and miracles to work.

"We had a tape recorder and put a switch under the seat cushion," said R.D. Lozier.

"When a kid would sit down, it would trip the switch and they would hear an actual ambulance run, complete with lights and sirens."

Dr. Bones, Lozier's skeleton on a bicycle, mirrored the children themselves on another bike,

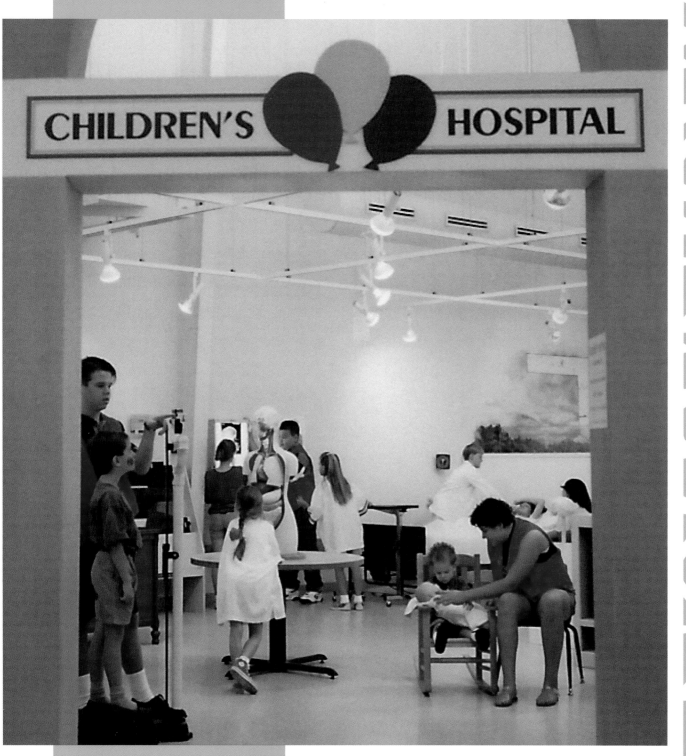

Children's Hospital later was replaced with a multi-million dollar hospital suite. *Courtesy Jacklyn Patterson Photography.*

teaching them about joints and bones. A ten-foot tall rag doll named Stuffie unzipped to remove and replace shaped fabric organs: lungs, liver and heart.

The Gentle Dental area was designed to teach children about the structure of the mouth and its working parts. Models showed healthy and unhealthy teeth so visitors could discover the importance of proper care of the mouth. Children could sit in the dental chair and see dentist's tools. Displays of primary and permanent teeth, incisors, cuspids and molars completed the dentist's office. Seminole dentist Dr. Jack Randolph donated the dental chair.

The museum's design team decorated with handprints in the Handi-Capable exhibit and masks and musical notes in the theater. In the school room they chose a big yellow ruler with the ABCs in chalk. The Bubble Room needed fish murals. The art room was decorated with shapes: circles, triangles and squares. The team used Homeland's colors in the grocery store after Homeland promised to sponsor it.

Small children and their parents could enjoy the "Tot Spot," a soft room filled with foam cushions for crawling and navigating. Rocking chairs and toys for the youngest children would make the area popular when the noise of the main hall became too much. Many of the items in the area were donated by Beta Sigma Phi, a local sorority.

One exhibit which did not last that long, but was hilarious in its implementation, was the Pink Cadillac.

During the museum's creation phase, Jasmine

and Melvin were in Europe, walking the streets of a small German city, and saw a pink plastic Cadillac in a store window. They went inside to inquire about buying the car for the Children's Museum.

The vehicle was a blow-up affair, with air pumped into several different compartments. It was big enough for two children to sit in the driver's seat. The problem was that the one in the window was the only one available.

"So we had to let the air out," Melvin said. "Jasmine and I went into the window of the store and jumped on it and rolled around on it for about 45 minutes to get the air out.

"By the time we finished, there was a huge crowd outside watching two crazy Americans on their stomachs and their backs rolling around on this pink Cadillac," Melvin said.

The car was folded and placed into a large box and hauled all over Europe by the Morans for the next couple of weeks until they finally had it shipped back home. The Cadillac was in the museum for a couple of years before being discarded.

Accumulation

accumulation (uh-kyoo-myuh-ley-shuhn), n.
act or state of accumulating; growth by continuous
additions, as of interest to principal

MODEL T

Wherever he went, Melvin talked about his project and more than once it seemed like there was someone in his audience who needed to hear his message.

In the summer of 1990, Senator David Boren spoke about the plan at the annual conference of the Oklahoma Independent Petroleum Association (OIPA), which was being held at Shangri-La Resort on Grand Lake.

"He spoke of a large abandoned building, previously occupied by an oilfield service company," said Claudean Greene, who attended the conference with her husband, David.

"He said that this museum would be a 'hands on' facility — no roped off displays, a 'climb in and make it work' kind of place for children of all ages."

Greene immediately thought of the 1921 Model T Ford, which had been sitting under wraps in her father's garage since his death the previous summer.

She discussed her idea with her family.

"I believe the building of the Model T was one of Dad's planned life events that he knew was supposed to occur toward the end of his life and, in his own way, he planned it, slow and deliberate," said Greene's brother, David Starrett.

It is his contention that their father, John Delbert Starrett, a chemical engineer for Phillips Petroleum, had spent a lifetime planning to build a facsimile of the first car he ever owned; the why, however, had never really occurred to any of his family.

Starrett said his father began the life-long process of building the car when he bought property

John Delbert Starrett dreamed of building a Model T. His family believes he worked toward that dream all his life. In the 1980s, at the age of 79, he began with this heap of scrap metal.

for the family home in Bartlesville in the 1940s. He built the home himself, laying cement blocks, mixing cement by hand, digging a full basement and water well, all by himself, and all with the cash he had on hand. The children played nearby, catching rides in the wheelbarrow between loads of cement blocks.

Slowly and systematically, all the while working and raising his family, John Starrett began to build and ultimately enlarge a machine shop with drill press, metal lathe, welding unit, industrial-sized air compressor and other tools that most people did not really understand. It was while David Starrett was in second grade that his father had a huge steel beam delivered that would eventually be used with a hoist to pull engines from cars, another step towards building the Model T.

About 1985, Greene said her father took a trip to Texas with a longtime friend, Brad Skinner, who was a collector of unrestored antique cars. He returned with a flatbed trailer stacked with scrap metal. When asked what he was going to do with it, he said, "That is my Model T; it needs a little work."

"It looked like Humpty Dumpty needing to be put back together again," said Greene's sister, Janice Starrett Banks.

Their father began securing old rusted Model T body parts, along with rotted wooden spoke wheels and other parts. He searched for parts in salvage yards, fields and swap meets. He made several trips to Hershey, Pennsylvania, to attend the fall classic car flea markets, an antique car buff's heaven. The

parts that needed the most work went to the shop and were sandblasted, welded and refurbished. The parts he could not find, he made himself.

"I remember Dad telling me that the finished body was actually from two different year models, but that they were compatible," Starrett said. "He could have made any year model parts work."

"His hands and fingers were big, but he could work with the teeniest items, like beads, buttons, screws or parts for his car," said Banks. "His sisters told us how, growing up on a farm in Kansas, he would have tea parties with them. He was always a gentle and caring man."

Greene said their father actually started building the car when he was 79 and completed it two years later.

"I wish I could remember all the details on the

car and the stories Dad told about how and where he found and collected each piece and part, the processes he went through to rebuild and revitalize each of them, and the completion of the car," Starrett said.

John Starrett's wife of 50 years, Pearl, died in December, 1987, of diabetes complications; he had nursed her during her final year. After that the car became a central part of his life. He loved talking about the car, "showing it off," and especially taking his friends and grandchildren on rides.

"It was like being in a parade," Greene said. "Everyone would wave and Dad would honk the horn." The family called the car "Chitty Chitty Bang! Bang!" after the classic 1968 children's movie.

Starrett shows off his completed Model T.

Starrett's daughters Janice Banks, above, and Claudean Greene delivered the Model T to the museum on a trailer. Director Tommy Mills and founder Melvin Moran help unload their prize.

John Starrett died in June, 1989, at the age of 83.

"One of the last memories I have of him as a very healthy man was working on the Model T," David Starrett said. "We were underneath the car putting needle bearings around the drive shaft. It was dirty, greasy and I had not known what a needle bearing was until Dad asked me to lend a hand for the tricky maneuver."

After his death, it was natural that the family agonized over what to do with his beloved car.

"It seemed a shame not to have the family and friends enjoy the car," Greene said. "We wanted to preserve it and at the same time have children enjoy it."

As soon as she heard of the museum project, Greene approached Jasmine, who gladly accepted the gift.

"My brother and sister were thrilled with the idea and we knew the plan would have pleased our dad," she said.

They loaned the Model T to the museum indefinitely. The sisters delivered the car on a trailer just before the museum opened.

"When they drove it in, they unhooked the battery cables," said Doyle Morris, who was in charge of maintenance at the new museum. "But one kid was cranking it and it putt-putted and almost started! After that we unhooked the crank."

Former Director Tommy Mills said he once found a child underneath, "fixing the engine."

Although the Starrett family was happy to give so many children a chance to enjoy their father's handiwork, it is not only the children who are attracted to the Model T. Seminole oil pioneer Bill Parks and his dear friend, Cynthia Williams, stop for a "ride" during his 80th birthday party at the museum.

As director, Marci found another child underneath, trying to fix the car.

"I was concerned about him hitting his head or perhaps dislodging some important part of the car," she said. "So I asked to see his mechanics license. Is there such a thing?

"He said he did not have one, so I told him I was sorry, only licensed mechanics could work on our car. He said okay and crawled out to play in another area. He was so cute!"

The car has been a "kid-magnet," everyone agrees.

"Lots of imaginary trips have been made behind that steering wheel," Greene said. "Melvin tells me it is one of the most photographed exhibits for visitors young and old."

"I know that Daddy is looking down on 'Chitty Chitty Bang! Bang!' smiling on how much joy came from his long and tireless work," Banks said.

Since then Greene has served on the board of directors and has participated in fundraisers, brick sales and quarterly meetings.

"My husband and I live in Bartlesville and own a small company, so time and distance keep me from being as active as I could be if it were closer to Seminole," she said.

She called Marci a "miracle worker" and commended Melvin and Jasmine for pursuing their vision.

"The Children's Museum truly is an Oklahoma treasure," Greene said.

Celebration

celebration (sel-uh-brey-shuhn), n.
an act of celebrating; the festivities engaged
in to celebrate something.

The Jasmine Moran Children's Museum officially
opened at 10:00 a.m. on January 23, 1993, exactly
four years and three months after the initial luncheon
at the Gusher Inn, beating the average museum
creation phase by eight months.

"At first I was concerned when Mel gave the
museum my name," Jasmine said. "I would have
preferred that it be called the Moran Museum."

But once again Melvin's personal friendship
with God directed the order of his life.

"We were in Colorado and I began having a
problem," Jasmine said. "With the altitude, my blood
pressure began dropping and would not respond to
medication. I was hospitalized. I became very ill and
the doctor said, 'I am losing her and I do not know
why. I have done everything I can to stop her blood
pressure from dropping.'"

"He said the only thing that might help was prayer. I am a firm believer in prayer," Melvin said.

"They had a little chapel in the hospital and Melvin went in and prayed," Jasmine said. "When he came back, the doctor said, 'A miracle has taken place. Her blood pressure has stopped dropping. I do not know if it was your prayer or our hope.'"

Jasmine stayed awhile longer in Colorado with their daughter and Melvin flew home.

"It was then that he announced that the museum would be named after me," Jasmine said. "I was aggravated at the time. I told him, 'Melvin, you might as well not have prayed. They only name things after people when they are dead. Now you have done it.'"

People visiting the museum will often look at the plaque with her name on it and say, "When did she die?"

"But I have teased him about that long enough, I guess," Jasmine said, laughing.

The museum opened to crowds of parents and children, all eager to see, to play, to learn. Cost per ticket was $2.50. The Saturday morning museum opening was preceded Friday evening with a 5:00 p.m. reception at the museum, followed by a banquet at 6:30 p.m. at Seminole State College. Dr. Jim Cook served as master of ceremonies and then U.S. Senator David L. Boren was guest speaker. Marci, Melvin and Tommy Mills also spoke and former State Secretary of Public Instruction Sandy Garrett was awarded a special commendation.

In her acceptance speech, she called the museum Melvin's "field of dreams" and paraphrased the line from the movie of the same name: "If Melvin builds it, they will come."

Director Tommy Mills remembered the grand opening.

"I was in shock that so many kids showed up," he said. "I had a generational problem, I think. I was brought up by very strict parents and we were strict on our children. We did not let them tear things up.

"At the opening, I learned that some of what we had was too fragile. The electric train, for example: the kids would take two engines and run them together. We had to put in a start button."

Prior to opening day, the board and staff had discussed what might be their biggest problem, but nobody thought about knobs and buttons.

"Children will pull a button off a machine and then they are scared so they put it in their pocket and take it home," Melvin said. "After opening day, we had lots of knobs and buttons missing, so we learned to have plenty of replacements on hand."

"We learned that kids run when they get excited," Mills said. "We put up speed limit signs. The staff learned how to deal with kids running: get in front of them and ask them to please slow down."

But the days working with children also were very fulfilling.

"Some of the most gratifying groups were the special ed kids," he said. "It was just special watching them. One child came to the hospital, picked up the stethoscope and started listening to his teacher's heart. He had been in a lot of hospitals.

"That still touches me."

Mills noticed that the children who came often usually played in the same exhibits for a period of time, then moved on.

"You could just see their interests broadening," he said.

Once open, though, it was not always easy to fill the museum with happy, playful children.

"I remember being open sometimes on a Sunday and there would not be 10 people there," said accountant Ann Biddy.

"We had a hard time convincing schools that it would be worth their while to drive to Seminole. But word of mouth helped. I think a lot of parents brought their kids and then told their schools that it was a good place for a field trip."

She also remembered a national television show being filmed there and broadcast on the FX Channel, as well as some features on Oklahoma City stations.

In January, 1996, Mills stepped down as director of the museum.

"I got wrapped up in that museum," he said. "After I left, I returned a couple of times, and decided I would be better off not to go back because I can remember it just like I like it.

"It was like being in love with someone and getting a divorce and still being in love with them. I have that weird feeling about the museum. I do not have any bitter feelings at all, but I would want to be involved again if I went back and I have too many fish to catch, too much mowing to do."

"After Tommy retired, I became convinced that Marci should become our director," Melvin said. "I remember going over to her home to visit with her and Dale and do whatever I could to convince her because I was certain that she would be terrific. And she has been more terrific than any of us ever imagined."

"I had to leave school," she said, and still gets a little teary when she thinks of all the children she had taught and the ones for whom she would no longer be there for. But at the museum, her opportunity to reach children is unparalleled.

"I felt safe to make the move, though, because we had this group of well-respected people who said we could do this," she said. "We had a committed support system. At no point did any of us say we cannot do this. There was no tone of doubt."

Since Marci needed to finish the school year, dedicated board member Zora Fowler was asked to fill in.

Fowler, then an instructor and vice president at Seminole State College, remembered being called to the president's office that day. Both she and President Jim Cook had been involved in the Jasmine Moran Children's Museum project almost since its inception. Both currently were board members and Fowler was serving as president of the executive committee.

"I remember that fateful day," she said. "Dr. Cook inquired if I had four hours to devote to being the interim executive director of the Children's Museum without affecting my teaching position or my family life.

"I said yes, because gullible me thought he meant four hours a week. What a shock to realize that I had committed to four hours a day for the next several months!"

Fowler took on the challenge, but quickly saw what a task she had set for herself.

"This was before e-mail, so I often received 10-plus faxes a day from Melvin asking me if particular tasks had been accomplished and/or giving me vital information to keep things running smoothly at the museum," she said.

Her duties also included traveling with Melvin to visit potential donors or board members.

"Those months were an interesting and challenging time," Fowler remembered. "It was certainly a learning opportunity, which helped me later as other opportunities presented themselves in my professional career."

She gladly relinquished the director's position when school was out that spring.

"It did not take me long to understand that Marci has a gift and a passion for the museum that cannot be duplicated," she said.

Marci found it was harder to leave the classroom than she thought.

"I was clearing out my desk," she said, as

she sat in her office at the museum. "I remember worrying if I was making the right decision. In the empty classroom, I saw the faces of the kids who had blessed my life. I knew nothing about running a business, which a museum is. I knew it was a chance to do something special for kids. I spotted the Bible on my desk and turned to Ecclesiastes: 'to everything there is a season.'

"I still miss the classroom to this day. Every retired teacher will tell you the same thing.

"But just today there was an anonymous letter praising our work here at the museum. And it felt like sunshine radiating from my soul."

Affirmation

affirmation (af-er-mey-shuhn), n.
the assertion that something exists or is true; the act or
an instance of affirming; state of being affirmed

Doyle Morris, who had started with the museum when it was hardly more than a dream, was holding open the door when the ribbon was cut on the museum. He stayed on for 14 more years as head of maintenance.

"My grandson Justin Parker was living with me at the time," Morris said. "They would let me take him to work with me. He would find things broken and either fix them himself or tell me."

Morris smiled when he remembered the buses pulling up outside the museum, all those little noses pressed flat against the windows.

Every day Melvin would be there looking at the comment book.

"I always tried to fix things by the next day," Morris said. "Otherwise someone would put it in the comment book and Melvin would see it."

From his home near Sportsmans Lake, Morris

can sit, braided hair laying to his waist over his overalls, and spin tales about the museum for hours.

"I remember that for a time, the alarm kept going off," he said. "Tommy kept getting awakened at 2:00 or 3:00 a.m. They thought someone was messing with the doors, but could not find anything."

One day Morris was working on the foot pedal of the airplane and found a cat hair. He began a search and uncovered a hole where a cat was entering the building at night. After the hole was patched, there were no more midnight burglar alarms.

For Morris and the rest of the staff, the museum has figured into every bit of history that occurred over the past 20 years.

"I watched the Oklahoma City bombing and the Twin Towers in New York City fall on the same little TV in the museum classroom," he said.

A few days after the Oklahoma City bombing, Morris found a Ryder rental truck parked outside the museum. The truck was similar to the one which held the explosives in the Murrah Federal Building bombing, roughly 60 miles away, on April 16, 1995.

"I poked around and went looking for a driver, but never found one," he said. "When I came back it was gone."

After the Oklahoma City bombing, memorial bricks were purchased by Marci's fourth grade class for all the children who died in the Murrah building's daycare center; they were placed next to the classroom exhibit.

"I usually laid the bricks on Monday when no one else was around," Morris said. "I put all the bricks Melvin bought in memory of someone between Homeland and the hospital. I called that Memory Lane."

"Selling the bricks was not an original idea, but it was mine," said accountant Ann Biddy. "I asked Melvin if we could do it and I researched where we could get the bricks and have them printed. Every

Doyle Morris was the museum's first Employee of the Year in 1996. He accepted the award from interim director, Zora Fowler.

time a shipment came in, Doyle and I would go over the spelling of each name and decide a place to put them. We tried to keep the families all together."

Biddy also said Morris was one of the museum's best assets.

"We felt we could go to him for anything," she said. "He had been there from the beginning, so he knew how everything was built."

Until his medical retirement in 2007, Morris laid every brick in the brick streets, including the one for a museum volunteer who died in an automobile accident. But to this day, he still does not have one for himself or his wife.

"I remember getting dizzy vacuuming bricks and reading those names upside down," he said.

His memories of the museum include his fight against the encroachment of pigeons, an attempted break-in and the continual and on-going repairs.

"Once a guy tried to break in by climbing onto the plane [the nose of which sticks out of the building]," Morris said. "He took off a plate, but there was a pipe there. If he had gone a little bit in either direction, he would have gotten in."

Another time someone broke into the shop and stole tools.

"We knew who it was because he had recently been fired from the museum," Morris said. "They found him hiding in his attic with the tools."

Morris' job of maintaining the exhibits was more than full time, and he remembers butting heads with the director more than once over overtime.

"Most people would not have stayed all night trying to get the camera running for the next day," he said. "I had no idea how to fix it, but I got a book and I got lucky. I would get in trouble for overtime, take my chewing and get it fixed. I could not leave it down. I hated an out-of-order sign. But sometimes the volunteers would put a sign up instead of calling me."

He said he "made my own job" because no one knew as much about the building as he did.

"I knew just how many screws everything had and where they were," he said.

Morris patched and repaired the damage done by inquiring little fingers day after day.

"I patched Dr. Bones until there was hardly anything left but screws," he said. "They bicycled until Dr. Bones' legs came off. I would tack them back together until Mondays [when the museum was closed] when I could do it right. Sometimes I would have to do a quick fix until something could be fixed permanently and it might last a month.

"The audiometer, the TDY phones for the deaf, they were always broken. The kids wore out five or six video cameras. The model train had to be fixed so they could not operate the switches and buttons."

Another time Morris had to get a ladder to get a kid down from the top of the slide on the climbing maze.

"They wanted to crawl up on the outside and hang there," he said.

"The museum is supposed to be hands-on, but

I learned quickly the kids would tear the stuff right off the walls.

"When I learned about easy anchor screws, I was so happy! They will screw anything into the drywall. Easy anchors, a screw gun and fishing line and I can fix anything."

Morris was sometimes called to fill in other places besides the maintenance which he loved.

"I loved giving train rides to the little mentally challenged kids," he said. "You could see the excitement on their faces and they would all say thank you."

He remembered giving train rides to jazz artist Wayman Tisdale and former Oklahoma First Lady Donna Nigh.

"The sprinklers came on and she got all wet," he said. "I thought I would lose my job, but she was not mad; she just laughed."

He would help out at the photo booth to keep the line moving.

"The kids loved taking pictures," Morris said. "Sometimes they would try to get five or six kids in there all at once. I wonder how many thousands of kids I photographed there."

Hundreds of times kids put their coins in the coin-mashing machine, then tried to use them in the dollar changer or parking meter, rendering the machinery inoperable every time.

"I would put them in my back pocket and they would end up in the washing machine," he said. In his home, there is an archway between the kitchen and living room that is lined with the mashed coins, all dug from his pockets or the washing machine, 14 years worth of them.

Morris is not the only museum staff member with stories to tell, both thrilling and heart-warming.

"That first year, I had a call in the gift shop," said Paula Anderson, the museum's accounts receivables clerk, who sometimes works in the gift shop.

"A woman called to ask if we still allowed photos to be taken in the museum. She said she had lost her child and the last memories she had of him were at the museum. She had enlarged the photos she took that day and hung them on the wall. She was encouraging her friend to bring a camera when she came with her children.

"She and I were both crying by the time that call ended," she said. "I still think of that call every time I sell a camera in the gift shop."

The gift shop was overseen by JaNene Day for many years after Vivian Mills left, and now is run by Tobie Rider.

"I cannot think of a better place to work," Day said. "It has been a great experience and I am thankful to be a part of it."

She tried to stock items that were fun and educational and often thinks about the little boy who decided the "Wacky Wiggler" looked too tasty.

"There were about 30 children in the gift shop," Day said. "A boy of about seven bit the 'Wacky Wiggler' and green liquid went everywhere. We had to shut everything down and clean it up."

She was frequently inspired, Day said, to see how some teachers would spend their own money to make sure every child got something from the gift shop.

"We try to keep a lot of inexpensive items so kids can afford to buy something and we keep extra change to help them complete their purchase if they do not have enough money," she added.

Marci talked about a family visiting with their autistic daughter, who seemed unable to participate in what was going on around her.

While the family played in the aquarium area, the autistic girl began watching other children in the Video Magic exhibit playing, "Honey, I Shrunk the Kids."

The museum's staff became close through day-to-day shared experiences and frequent celebrations.

"The youth volunteer motioned for her to come over and she joined in," Marci said. "When her mother found her, she rushed over to the volunteer and said, 'How did you get her to do that? It is the first time she has ever come out of her shell this way.'"

She also tells of children who liked the courtroom exhibit so much they are now studying to be lawyers, one who liked the hospital exhibit so much that she is now in medical school and one whose family of doctors and lawyers were shocked when their child decided in the Homeland exhibit that she wanted to become a grocery clerk.

"Encouraging children to role play in various jobs and professions really works," Melvin said.

One child told the staff that he wanted to be a

doctor until he came to the museum and proclaimed "Now I want to be a dinosaur guy."

The guest books are full of fascinating comments about the museum. One family from England wrote that it was worth crossing the Atlantic just to see the museum.

Success stories are punctuated by stories of things that should not have happened. But even in those, the museum seems to have been provided some divine protection.

"I got a call on a Sunday afternoon," Marci said. "The ultralight plane donated by Jim Goff, which hangs and rotates over the center of the museum, became dislodged. It fell once and then again in the dead center of the museum, where a lot of children play."

Fortunately, the plane caught by a tiny thread until the museum staff could remove the visitors and section off the area.

Another time a boy climbed up the outside of the climbing maze, using his sharp-toed cowboy boots to unhook the s-hooks as he went. As he called down to his mother, "Look at me!" a youth volunteer ran up the maze to pull him in before a terrible accident might have occurred.

Once a school group left, but everyone was not in their proper seat on the bus. "This was a time when there was a real need for 'No Child Left Behind,'" joked Marci.

The child, a little boy, continued having the time of his life until after 4:00 p.m. when he was

Although the ultralight plane donated by Jim Goff still hangs above the museum's main gallery, a near accident had the staff scurrying to protect children and secure the plane.

discovered unattended by the museum staff. Marci was called downstairs.

"We called the school, but no one was there," she said.

The child was not frightened and the museum staff gave him soda and candy, brought him up into Marci's office to watch cartoons — basically gave him the royal treatment.

Meanwhile Marci and the staff were agonizing on how best to handle the situation. They called the Oklahoma Highway Patrol to see if they could intercept the bus as it headed back to the school. It was May 3, 1999.

"All our troopers are out handling the storms," dispatch told them. "We will see if we have anyone in that area."

The bus was intercepted and someone sent to pick up the missing child. They questioned the child on why he did not stay with the group. He told them he was having too much fun.

When the school representative began to admonish the child, Marci, the former teacher, came to his defense.

"I reminded them that the adult in charge of the boy was the one who should be chastised," she said. She asked why the bus left when the child did not answer roll call ... but got no answer.

"They hurried away, but the boy whose pockets were filled with treats looked back at me and smiled," Marci remembered. "That made my day."

It is not only children who learn from the Jasmine Moran Children's Museum. Many times museum builders from other states come for pointers. Astronaut Tom Stafford and the director of his museum visited for ideas on hands-on exhibits. The Children's Museum staff was instrumental in helping the Commerce [Texas] Children's Museum. The creators of Leonardo's Warehouse visited and sought advice before opening in Enid. Founders of a toy and action museum in Pauls Valley, some from Fort Worth, Texas, from Stillwater, and from the Gaylord-Pickens Oklahoma Heritage Museum in Oklahoma City all visited and asked for tips and ideas from the Seminole museum builders.

"We have had visitors from a number of states, and one from Israel," Melvin said. "Her sole destination was Seminole. She spent four days here, including two days visiting the museum, and we invited her to attend a two-day retreat during her visit."

Once a delegation of 17 Chinese children, 10 to 15 years of age, visited the United States with their teachers for several weeks. They arrived in California and visited Disneyland and other California attractions. They came to Oklahoma and toured the state, including the Children's Museum. They traveled to Washington and visited the nation's landmarks.

Shortly after their return to China, the staff at the Jasmine Moran Children's Museum received a letter from the teachers telling them that the children voted the Children's Museum as America's No. 1 attraction.

AFFIRMATION

In 1995, the museum held its first annual spring egg hunt, a free event which continues annually to date.

"We hide almost 10,000 eggs, each one filled with a special prize," Marci said. "Our acreage is speckled with brightly colored eggs."

It takes hours to fill the eggs and more hours to creatively hide the eggs. It takes only two minutes to find the eggs.

"When the whistles blow, it is like the Oklahoma land run," Marci said. "We even have some 'sooners,' usually in the form of parents."

In October, the museum's free Great Pumpkin Event attracts hundreds of costumed children and their caregivers.

"Many of these children might not otherwise be able to afford admission," Marci said.

In addition to the free events, donors have given money to fund scholarships for children who could not otherwise afford to attend.

In 2003, the museum celebrated its ten-year anniversary with a huge event in the Haney Center, Seminole State College. Melvin and Marci presented a history of the museum at a banquet and talked about the future. Former Governor George Nigh was the featured speaker. Others included former U.S. Senator David Boren, BancFirst President Gene Rainbolt and then State Superintendent of Public Instruction Sandy Garrett.

"I donated to the project because I did not know how to say 'no,'" said Rainbolt. "I never

Jazzy's Egg Hunt draws hundreds of children each spring. *Courtesy Lesley Werner/Seminole Producer.*

expected the museum to actually open."

"I was given a tour of this large empty building and was told, 'This exhibit will be here and this exhibit will be there,'" said Garrett. "I said to myself, 'Sure it will.' I did not expect the museum to ever open either."

But open it did and it has been an asset for people of all ages since. In fact, the same year the museum celebrated its tenth anniversary, it also was named by Governor Brad Henry as one of his official inaugural event sites. Nearly 1,000 visitors enjoyed the free all-day event. Clowns, balloons and performances by Lyric Theater actors highlighted the festivities.

Governor Brad Henry
named the Jasmine Moran
Children's Museum as
one of the venues for his
inaugural events in 2003.

Continuation

continuation (kuhn-tin-yoo-ey-shuhn), n.
the act or state of continuing; the state of being continued;
extension or carrying on to a further point

ONGOING FUNDRAISING

Just because the museum was open and successful did not mean the founders could relax. The need for ideas, enthusiasm and for fundraising continued as the museum grew.

The Morans continue to be intimately involved in the museum's fundraising and expansions. Melvin visits the museum every day, interviewing visitors and looking over the comments in the guestbook. The staff seems to love him, always smiling, talking to him, offering him drinks and food.

During the early 1990s, the museum coordinated with Seminole State College to hire grant writer Dr. Carmen Notaro. Grants he wrote included a U.S. Department of Energy and Transportation grant for the Safety Town exhibit and $498,000 for a new train track; two grants from the Institute of Museum and Library Services in Washington, D.C., for operations; grants from Exxon-Mobil and Eaton Corporation; and, with the help of a dedicated board member, the Ronald McDonald House Charities.

He also initiated the Legacy Program, where board members, staff and the community contribute on a monthly basis toward the museum's endowment fund. The fund currently totals $3.7 million.

Even though Carmen Notaro is no longer employed by the museum, he still believes Melvin's daily visits to the museum are an important way of learning the demographics of his visitors.

"A good man wants to know all about the persons who visit his home," Notaro said. "Reading the guest book is what Melvin does. It is not surprising that many benefits accrued from this habit."

Notaro also commented that Melvin's daily visits with Marci illustrate his respect for her and provides the ideal, non-threatening opportunity to share ideas and to brainstorm.

Notaro's salary is not the only way Seminole State College has stayed involved with the museum throughout the years. Current President Dr. Jim Utterback and numerous members of the faculty and staff either have served or currently serve on the museum board. The athletic teams, particularly the Trojan baseball team and girls' softball and basketball teams, volunteer annually to help with seasonal events. Several Presidential Leadership Scholars and members of the Neil Molleur Volunteer Scholarship Program work at the museum. And SSC has provided student workers through partnerships such as the national AmeriCorps program.

Although the museum is able to generate almost 75 percent of its operating budget, ongoing support is necessary, and Marci and Melvin are well aware of that fact. The average generated by most museums is 20 to 25 percent.

Much ongoing support had come from Southwestern Bell. David Lopez, who served as president of Southwestern Bell in Oklahoma from early 1995 until 1998, was a big supporter and continued to support the museum after his move to San Antonio; he has since returned to the state and re-engaged his involvement.

"I was so impressed," Lopez told Paul Lambert in a 2006 interview. "I had been on the board of the Austin Children's Museum; this was a modest museum compared to what Melvin was doing and was envisioning. I became very enthused."

Lopez credits Melvin's abilities as a salesman and a humorist, making him irresistible when Melvin is enthusiastic about a project. Southwestern Bell gave an initial donation, then increased their support over the years.

"Initially I wondered how the museum could draw sufficient crowds to Seminole," Lopez said. "It was difficult in Austin! But it was a different concept here, with the traveling exhibits and other things. It took root. Perhaps the small town people are just comfortable there. But people from all over the state wanted it to succeed."

One thing he noticed early on was the materials presented were effective, but not professionally prepared.

"They were saving money," Lopez said. "Contributions were going to benefit the kids, not to print slick brochures. Overhead was minimized. They used resources and people in the community and that worked beautifully for the kids."

In 1998, working with board member Ron Howell's Tulsa consulting firm State Source, the idea came for annual fundraisers, in the form of golf tournaments and tribute banquets. They decided to alternate between Tulsa and the Oklahoma City metro area for the events. The result was a tribute

Melvin Moran and Oklahoma's First Lady Kim Henry visit with Jasmine Award winner Barry Switzer. Switzer won the Jasmine Award in 2009.

banquet in Tulsa one year and a celebrity golf tournament in the Oklahoma City metro area the following year.

In odd years, beginning in 1999, the tribute event would honor a well-known Oklahoman who had done good and positive things for children. They would be presented with a "Jasmine" Award. Benefactor awards also were planned.

The first banquet was held at the DoubleTree Hotel in Tulsa and subsequent banquets have been hosted at the Southern Hills Marriott Hotel, until 2011 when Robert Henry received the award at the National Cowboy and Western Heritage Museum in Oklahoma City.

"The principal reason we changed to the Southern Hills Marriott is because we have a reception prior to the banquet," Melvin explained. "The DoubleTree did not have a suitable place for the reception that was near the ballroom. In fact it was in a different building and was too time consuming for our guests to go from one building to the other. At the Southern Hills Marriott, the reception is on the second floor, just steps down to the first floor ballroom."

The same held true for the National Cowboy and Western Heritage Museum, formerly the Cowboy Hall of Fame.

The Jasmine Award was designed by Oklahoma artist Kim Walker Ray, an award-winning artist whose works are found in collections throughout the United States.

In 2007 George and Donna Nigh won the celebrated Jasmine Award, created by Oklahoma sculptor Kim Walker Ray. They are congratulated by Jasmine and Melvin Moran and Governor Brad Henry and First Lady Kim Henry.

In December, 2001, Ray was awarded a Master of Fine Arts degree with an emphasis in figurative sculpture, a program re-established at the University of Oklahoma by David Boren in 1997.

Her creation of the Jasmine Award came from several visits to the Children's Museum and discussions with the staff on the importance of play and imagination in the lives of children.

In the Jasmine Award, she used a depiction of a young doctor listening to a puppy's heartbeat, an archaeologist contemplating the age of dinosaurs and an aviator piloting a trans-Atlantic flight   all hands-on professions children can imagine and role-play at the Children's Museum.

Ray has public sculptures at the Sam Noble Oklahoma Museum of Natural History in Norman, the Charles M. Russell Center and the Donald Reynolds Performing Arts Center, both at the University of Oklahoma, as well as a bronze relief sculpture of Melvin and Jasmine Moran at the Children's Museum.

The first recipient of the Jasmine Award, on March 30, 1999, was then Oklahoma First Lady Cathy Keating. Mike Turpen and Burns Hargis, well-known political commentators from the television show "FlashPoint," served as masters of ceremonies. Most years, former Governor George Nigh has served as master of ceremonies; the only exception was the year when he and his wife, Donna, were honored. At that time Robert Henry served as emcee.

"After the first banquet, probably 20 people informed me that the event lasted far too long,"

Melvin said. After that all speakers were given a strict time limit.

Melvin almost missed the first banquet; two weeks prior to the banquet, he was diagnosed with aggressive prostate cancer. He urged the doctor to perform immediate surgery. But the doctor convinced him that he could delay the surgery for a month without serious threat, so he was able to attend the banquet.

In even-numbered years, the annual fundraiser is a golf tournament held in June, followed by a dinner and auction.

The first, held in 2000, was at Oak Tree Golf Course in Edmond. Many of the others have been held at the Jimmie Austin University of Oklahoma Golf Course in Norman. In 2012, the event was moved to the Jimmie Austin Municipal Golf Course in Seminole.

"Almost every major elected office holder in Oklahoma has participated in our celebrity golf tournaments," Melvin said.

"Where else but in Oklahoma would state government almost shut down for several hours to benefit the children of Oklahoma?" Marci asked.

Again espousing the theory that the museum has divine assistance, Melvin said, "Every year some of the team sponsors ask about our contingency plans in case it rains. And I say, 'We do not have any because it will not.' And it never has."

Modification

modification (mod-uh-fi-key-shuhn), n.
an act or instance of modifying; the state of being modified;
partial alteration; a modified form; variety.

NEW EXHIBITS

In the beginning there was no lunch room, a need which organizers recognized quickly.

"The first busload of children arrived and they said, 'We have brought sack lunches; where will we eat them?'" Melvin said. "We had never thought about that. Tommy did the only thing he could do. He put them on the floor in the various exhibit areas."

"We were feeding kids all over the museum," Doyle Morris said.

"We tried to schedule their lunches so they would not all be trying to find a place to eat at the same time," said accountant Ann Biddy.

The lunch room was the museum's first expansion. The Sarkeys Foundation funded a 2,000-square foot extension where the energy exhibit currently is.

"The schools could order lunches from McDonald's," Morris said. "Those little kids from Antlers or other far out places would see those little

Happy Meals and their eyes would light up as much as they did about anything else in the museum. They were so tickled and excited."

Morris laughed when he remembered that the leftover meals were just left behind.

"They were going to throw them out, so Tony [Lenora] and I would eat them," he said. "We ate so many Happy Meals! You can make a pretty good burger if you put about 10 of those little pieces of meat on one bun."

The staff enjoyed the kindness of many visitors to the museum.

"People were always bringing us food," Morris recalled. "I remember Daisy Mae Robinson bringing us goodies. Once she brought us a rum cake. We did not know she had put rum in it and poured about a fifth on top.

"I had quit drinking back in '94, but I had two pieces..."

The first lunchroom was followed by seven other expansions to date.

Today the children eat their lunch in the 6,000-square foot Roesler Hall, the museum's second expansion, completed in 1999 with partial funding by Dennis and Leilani Roesler of Seminole. The museum staff ferries lunch boxes and ice chests to the lunch room on four-tiered trollies.

Roesler Hall was also the site of the third expansion — a huge climbing maze and the Waterworks exhibit.

The 18-foot tall climbing maze is built with five miles of web-like cables strung together with 12,000 s-hooks. Occasional play platforms give children places to explore, and a long, closed slide serves as an exit. The slide was added later when traffic jams suggested kids needed another way out.

"This exhibit was mostly financed by Ronald McDonald House Charities, through my former fraternity brother, Irv Klein," Melvin said.

The idea for the maze came to Marci when she attended the Association of Children's Museums

Conference in Indianapolis. It was built by Tom Luckey, architect and principal owner of Luckey's Climbers, which builds climbing mazes all over the world.

"Tom Luckey brought in a friend who painted a dragon on the underside of the climbing maze," said Dale Donaho. "Later someone came in and wanted to know who painted it. It looked like the work of someone famous who had just dropped out of sight."

No one at the museum can remember the name of the artist. Morris, who headed maintenance at the museum for 14 years, said the dragon's seven pairs of golden eyes actually were not painted on, but came in a box.

The water exhibit came after Marci saw a similar one at a conference in Indianapolis.

"Their museum was 350,000 square feet and the kids spent two hours at the water exhibit," Marci said.

Keith Shaw, who continues to serve as project manager anytime a new exhibit or expansion is planned, enlisted the help of several local companies and Seminole engineer George Garbutt.

"Goff helped with some of the plastic inserts, Seminole Chemical participated with the pump and filtration," Shaw remembered. "The oak came from a sawmill north of Prague. George contributed back some of his time and expertise."

"It is our recollection that Indianapolis paid $100,000 for their exhibit," Melvin said. "Our total cost was $35,000."

The 12-foot tall climbing maze opened in Roesler Hall in 1999 with five miles of weblike cable. *Courtesy Sharon Wallace/Seminole Producer.*

Movable channels and locks move water through passageways children set up. Different water levels and tiny falls make for interesting duck races and children can crawl under the troughs and basins and come up inside the play area with water tables all around them.

The fourth expansion, in 2000, was Jasmine's Ark and the first riding train.

Jasmine's Ark is located outside the museum and named for her because of Jasmine's intense love for animals.

"Jasmine and I were driving to Oklahoma City one day and saw the boat for sale near a roadside," Melvin said. The boat had been built by the Amish

PVC pipe and fittings are used to move water to where is needed.

community. The Morans thought the children would enjoy it and so it was bought and placed on the museum grounds.

"This is a 'Titanic' photo opportunity for many young visitors," Marci said.

The museum's first train ride came about because of Melvin's memory of how much his small children had enjoyed the old Seminole Lions Club's train in Municipal Park.

Several years after the museum opened, he heard there was a riding train at an estate sale in Seminole County. He thought it was that same Lions Club train, although it turned out not to be. Tommy Mills, who was the museum director at the time, went to the auction and purchased the train, which did not run. It held only 14 children and no adults and had 600 feet of track.

The train was stored in the garage of the museum's then president, Harry Coates, and forgotten by all but one person. Coates' son, Eddie, kept reminding his father until finally Coates took the train to his sheet metal shop and had it repaired.

The restored train was so popular it ran 120 miles a month, 600 feet at a time.

"Jim Whitt was the driver," said Doyle Morris. "He drove until those little wheels gave out. Someone gave me a train book and I learned to work on it. I bought little wheels from Chicago."

The episode is memorialized by the mural in Roesler Hall. There is a train mural by April Ledbetter Jones near the door leading out to the train station, and features a young man they all call "Engineer Eddie," after Eddie Coates, whose persistence was responsible for the restoration of the small train.

When the train finally gave out, a 17-page, single-spaced grant by Dr. Carmen Notaro to the U.S. Department of Transportation brought funding for tracks and a station. Separate funding was necessary for a new train.

"Over the years, we made several fundraising presentations to the Sonic Corporation in Oklahoma City," Melvin said. "Each presentation was rewarded with a grant of $2,000 or $3,000."

In 2001, while fundraising for the new train, Melvin and Marci made another visit to Sonic, hoping for another $2,000 or $3,000.

They visited with vice president Nancy Robertson, who asked what the new train would be called. Using a suggestion from her husband, Dale, Marci asked, "How does SuperSonic Express sound?"

Robertson responded with a grant of $50,000.

With the Children's Museum, one success just seemed to lead to another, as with the grant from the Ad Astra Foundation.

A year before the SuperSonic Express was funded, the museum submitted a grant application to the Ad Astra Foundation, but it was unsuccessful.

"The trustees of the Ad Astra Foundation are Dick and Jeanette Sias," Melvin said. "In the rejection letter we received, it was explained to us that this foundation was founded to advance music and arts,

The Oklahoma Tourism Commission got a ride on the SuperSonic Express during a 2007 meeting at the museum. Safety Town is in the background and Jasmine's Ark sits off to the right.

especially music. We were rejected because our grant request had no connection to music."

The museum was encouraged to try again if they ever hosted a musical event.

A year later, Jasmine and Melvin attended a social event in the Oklahoma City home of board member Sandy Meyers and her husband, Stewart. The Siases were there and, as Jasmine visited with Dick Sias, she mentioned the new train.

Dick Sias said his grandson loved trains.

"Will your train have a whistle on it?" he asked.

"I imagine it will," said Jasmine.

"Will it have a bell?" he asked.

"I imagine it will have a bell as well," she responded.

"Whistles and bells are musical," Sias said. "Send me a grant application!"

They did and the Ad Astra Foundation responded with a generous check.

The new 16-guage diesel train was found in Chicago the following year, and Marci and Dale went to Chicago to see and purchase the train from Custom Locomotive. It has three cars, one of them handicap accessible, and takes 51 passengers on a half-mile trip through the newly-landscaped Henderson Nature Park on the museum's north side.

During the building of the tracks for the new train, it was decided that the train should go through a tunnel.

"We got an eight-foot high culvert and covered it with dirt," Keith Shaw said. "We drilled cross ties like a trestle. One day they were using a cutting torch to put up big metal doors and a spark hit the cross ties. I got a call, 'Keith, we have a fire.'

"By the time I got there, the fire department was there and they had already cut the lock on the gate and were getting ready to drive these big trucks across the tracks to put out the fire; it was just a little fire in the cross tie." He was able to stop them before the heavy machinery damaged the tracks.

The railroad depot, where passengers line up for their train ride, is a replica of the charming little depot in Dougherty, Oklahoma. On hot days, a cooling mist is blown from the ceiling, refreshing adults and delighting children.

The train and Safety Town were the fifth

expansion, completed in 2002.

"Our daughter and nephew had gone to Safety Town at Sooner Fashion Mall when we lived in Norman," said Marci's husband, Dale Donaho, who, until his recent retirement, was an instructor at Gordon Cooper Technology Center.

"That is what we set out to build, but as we got into it, Marci wanted it to be more functional and a place where kids could spend time. So I sat down with a student from Gordon Cooper and gave him a plot of the property. The concept grew larger. I designed the buildings and the student drew them

Congressman Dan Boren and his family get ready to board the train at the museum's depot during a visit in May, 2012. With Boren are Hannah and Jace Heupel, Andrea, Hunter and Jana Boren and Dawn Heupel.

up. It saved a great deal of money."

Safety Town encompasses 17 structures, street lights, directional signs and a gazebo, all constructed by students at Gordon Cooper Technology Center, using materials purchased with a grant from the Oklahoma Department of Transportation.

"The Gordon Cooper instructors used Safety Town as a method to teach various technical skills that will last them a lifetime," said Marci.

The roofs were donated by Coates Roofing and Central Sheet Metal. Local wrecker service owner Terry Howard and truck company owner Ronnie Allison hauled all the houses from Gordon Cooper. Seminole oilman Bill Parks provided tiny tanks for a small gas station. The Safety Town Schoolhouse was named in memory of board member Anne Zarrow.

The exhibit includes curriculum to teach children about areas of safety.

"Safety Town has posed some challenges to us," Donaho said. "We could use more staff and volunteers."

Donaho's relationship with Gordon Cooper Technology Center helped with the planning of the museum parking lot. He asked a CAD program instructor for help; the teacher put a student on it and a lot of money was saved when the parking lot was designed.

"Gordon Cooper has been a good partner," Donaho said.

The grounds and parking lot were landscaped by Cai Levy, the "creative team" member who by this time had taken a Master Gardener course and started a landscaping business, called Lady Bug, with her friend Darlene Wallace. As soon as funding was available they put in flower beds, focusing on visually stimulating plants, like geometrics, fuzzy, shiny, smooth plants and those with interesting smells or textures. In the parking lot, they used more native plants.

Prior to the opening, the museum had been able to purchase an additional seven and a half acres on the west side, bringing their holdings to 15 acres.

The north side of the museum held a small body of water and a trash dump that the museum founders knew could be an asset, but the work involved seemed daunting. Although part of the area did not belong to the museum, those riding the train got a birds-eye view of the dump and swamp. Keith Shaw got permission from the adjacent landowner to doze the old dump and then leveled the whole area.

"When we got ready to clean up the north side, we found that the tire shop that had been behind Power Transmission had been using a pit back there to dispose of tires," Marci said.

She asked Seminole State College's legendary baseball coach Lloyd Simmons and his team to help.

"Goodyear paid us a dollar a tire, which we gave to the SSC baseball program," she said. "I will never forget that day. It was so hot and Coach Simmons was out there in a nice silk shirt and slacks with a drink in one hand and a burrito in the other, watching.

"I asked if we could get the players some water and he said 'no'.

"Goodyear sent a trailer and it left here full."

In 2002 and 2003, Rose and Kenneth Henderson, owners of Seminole's historic Grisso Mansion, spent 15 months landscaping the area into a nature park, at no charge to the museum.

The Hendersons first became involved with the museum in 1999. Kenneth Henderson, a former pharmacist turned real estate developer, had a 1,000-acre ranch and non–profit wildlife refuge near Chandler, Oklahoma. When Melvin heard about it, he decided to bring the museum board out for one of their meetings. Afterwards, he asked Henderson to serve on the museum board. Not long afterwards, the Hendersons purchased the historic Grisso Mansion and became Seminole residents.

After moving to Seminole in 2001, the Hendersons were able to become even more involved with the museum. When the SuperSonic train track was finished in 2002, it became painfully obvious that the train would take the children on a tour of the north side of the museum — currently a dump.

"Melvin mentioned a lake on the north side of the property that the train went around," Kenneth Henderson said. "I went back there to look at it and it was just an overgrown farm pond that needed to be cleaned up. I have always enjoyed landscaping.

I visited with Melvin and Marci and expressed interest in working on that and they were very receptive."

Though the arguments have sparkled with humor, the lake/pond has been one of the few sources of contention between Marci and Melvin.

"While Marci has referred to this luxurious and splendid body of water as a 'pond,' I have always referred to this same area as a 'lake,'" said Melvin. "I have said to Marci, 'We need to think big.' And I have threatened to start referring to this wonderful wet area as a 'sea.'"

Melvin said they finally had agreed to call it a small lake, but said he suspected that sometimes when he was not around Marci still called it a pond and that he still forgets and calls it a lake sometimes.

Marci, however, said she had never agreed to call it a small lake.

"It is not that I don't want to think big," she said. "It is just that sometimes I have to be the reality person of the team. Museums are purveyors of truth, after all. If we were in a desert wasteland somewhere, I do suppose our pond would seem like a lake; but to Oklahomans, this is a pond... a nice upscale pond, though."

According to an internet search, the difference between a pond and a lake is not the difference in size, but in depth. A pond has a photic zone through its entire length and width; in other words, plants could potentially grow all across its surface or below its surface. A lake, however, is aphotic — the sun cannot penetrate to the bottom, therefore plants cannot grow over or below it.

"We did have water lilies growing in the pond at one time, which covered the eastern area," Marci said. "But to lay this puppy to rest, I vote to call it a 'body of water.'

"We really do have a lot of fun 'agreeing to disagree,'" she continued. "That is what makes working together a lot of fun: lots of laughter and crazy discussions!"

"After working with Marci for 22 years for the benefit of the Children's Museum, if a disagreement on what to call our body of water, it really is a lake, is our biggest point of contention, I think we have done pretty well," Melvin said.

Their hilarious discussions on the "body of water" did not slow down Kenneth Henderson when he got started landscaping. Working with his employee Jose Gomez, Henderson developed a plan, then went to work.

"First we needed to clean it up," he said. "The overflow system was a boggy, trashy area. We brought in a lot of dirt to fill that in properly. There were multiple dump truck loads and a lot of dozer work. The dam had to be reworked. We cut out scrub trees, some of which were damaging the dam."

Some funding was secured to help with the project, which was estimated to have been worth about $300,000 had Henderson not donated his time and labor.

They put in more than 30,000 square feet of sod, built a rock creek for overflow on the west side, lined and bridged it. Every rock was laid by hand.

"Star Sims built a bridge to the island and I put the wood on it," Kenneth said. "Then we were able to clean up the island."

"When we put in the bridge, Donaho drove the sky track and Rose and I were holding and steadying the bridge while he put it in place," Marci said.

"It was only the second time I had run a sky track," Donaho said. "We borrowed it from Harry Coates and when he came up, it was leaning over so far it would have fallen if anybody had pushed it."

Mature trees were bought and planted next.

"They were planted in July," Henderson said. "It was not a good time, but we got a good price from a nursery going out of business and have kept most of them alive."

Waterfalls and bronze statues completed the landscaping. On the east side, water is pumped from the lake and down the waterfall of donated rocks.

"His name was Big Al," Henderson said. "He donated all the rocks in the waterfall, and all the large rocks that you will see in that area. Jose and I helped him load them and we placed them."

A large fountain was placed in the center of the pond to circulate water and prevent algae growth.

After the bridge was placed, Henderson could clean up and landscape the little island. They brought in swans, ducks and geese for the lake, put in corn feeders and built them houses. They built and anchored rafts, where one might see turtles sunning on any given day.

The Hendersons built and bought 28 birdhouses, all different types for different kinds of birds. They planted a butterfly garden of more than 100 butterfly-attracting plants. The bronze statue in that area is of a little girl with a butterfly. There are a total of 10 bronze children in the garden, and some bronze birds. Where the old dump had been on the north side, there is a bronze of three children and a flagpole. An arbor, covered in summer by trumpet vine, welcomes visitors to the area recently named by the board "Henderson Nature Park."

To ride the train through the nature park and outdoor exhibits, visitors exit through the lunch room into a graveled area with outdoor picnic tables and a wood and plastic play station, a place to get some fresh air and blow off steam before riding the train.

"Jasmine and I and our family were on vacation at Whitefish, Montana, and there was a fair with booths selling all kinds of items," Melvin said. "One of the booths was manned by folks from Idaho who sold elaborate play stations."

The Morans wanted to buy a play station; later Marci contacted the company and chose the specific components for their play station.

Returning from the train ride, visitors will climb over the train tunnel for a walk to the Centennial

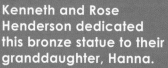

Kenneth and Rose Henderson dedicated this bronze statue to their granddaughter, Hanna.

"Hanna"
Statuary gifted to the Children's Museum by Kenneth and Rose Henderson in honor of their granddaughter, Hanna Levi, born August 17, 2004.

maze, the museum's sixth expansion.

In 2004, the Morans decided they wanted a maze similar to the ones Jasmine visited at castles while growing up in England. Keith Shaw, Marci and her husband, Dale, took a trip to Coconut Grove, Florida.

"Theirs was the size of a football field," Marci said.

Donaho recalled that it was cloudy outside that day and they got lost in the maze.

"That is when we decided to put our paneled walls three feet off the ground," he said.

"That is what Dale needed to crawl out," Shaw added.

"Marci wisely chose not to use hedges because of upkeep," Melvin said.

Although there are architects who build mazes, Dale Donaho was able to use an Excel program on his computer and drew the maze, with movable panels so it can be changed periodically. The front is flanked by tall silver knights, purchased and hauled in from Mexico by Rose and Kenneth Henderson; with the moat and turrets, the maze has a castle theme.

The 12,000-square-foot maze was funded by a bequest from Iowa schoolteacher, Paula Timmerman, and the Oklahoma Centennial Commission.

"Paula Timmerman came to the museum almost by accident with her granddaughter," Melvin said. "We never knew when she was there, but she was so impressed with the museum that, when she got home, she put the museum in her will."

Oklahoma's First Lady Kim Henry cuts the ribbon on the museum's castle maze funded in 2004 by a bequest from Iowa schoolteacher Paula Timmerman. Included in the festivities were Dale Donaho, Jasmine Moran, Nathylee Whitley, Betty Smith, Henry, Jim Smart, J. Blake Wade and Melvin Moran.

Tall silver knights were purchased and transported from Mexico for the castle maze by Rose and Kenneth Henderson. Melvin Moran is pictured at the entryway to the castle maze. *Courtesy of Jacklyn Patterson Photography.*

After Timmerman's death, Marci was notified of the bequest and invited the family to come to the museum to discuss what the $25,000 might be used for. They loved the idea of the castle maze. Their money was used as seed money, and they were joined by the Oklahoma Centennial Commission, because of the maze's uniqueness and educational components. A plaque inside the maze memorializes the Timmerman family's donation.

"The maze works beautifully," Donaho said. "It gives the children a chance for self-discovery but is low maintenance and uses very little staff involvement."

The seventh expansion, begun in 2005 and opened in 2008, was the Kim Henry Science Works wing, which includes a healthcare exhibit. The audio-kinetic exhibit is placed in the entryway to the new wing.

The healthcare exhibit was a joint project among five of Oklahoma's major healthcare providers. Henry, then First Lady of Oklahoma, was instrumental in bringing all the participants of the $500,000 project together.

"Well, that was not my puzzle," Henry said. "I just put two pieces together."

Melvin said Henry asked to be given something to do for the museum and he mentioned adding a surgical suite to the Hospital Exhibit.

"I asked him how much it would cost and he said about $100,000," Henry said.

She asked him if he knew Stanley Hupfeld,

the former CEO of Integris Health. Because Melvin did not, Henry offered to make an appointment for Marci and Melvin to meet Hupfeld in her office at the State Capitol. When Marci and Melvin spoke of the museum, Hupfeld said he could not make any kind of commitment until he actually visited the museum. An appointment was made for him to tour.

"When we left him, I told Melvin, 'We got it!'" Henry said. Sure enough when Hupfeld visited the museum, Henry said his remarks were, "You are not thinking big enough."

"I have never heard anybody tell Melvin Moran he does not think big enough!" she said, laughing. Integris not only gave $100,000, but helped contact four other healthcare companies — Mercy Health System of Oklahoma and OU Medical Center in Oklahoma City; St. Francis Health Care System in Tulsa; and SSM Health of Oklahoma, which encompasses St. Anthony and McBride Bone and Joint in Oklahoma City; and Unity Hospital in Shawnee — for $100,000 each. Kim Henry and Governor Brad Henry hosted a dinner for the donors at the Governor's Mansion to seal the deal and allow Melvin, Jasmine and Marci to thank the new contributors.

But the new healthcare exhibit would take up quite a bit of space, which currently was limited at the museum. Somehow they needed to expand, and before long the forces that some may call destiny — and others may call the will of Melvin — brought along funding for a new 8,400 square-foot, two-story wing. The major funder for this construction was Oklahoma City attorney Reggie Whitten.

Whitten had grown up in Seminole, graduating from Seminole High School in 1973. There was no Children's Museum there then to motivate him, but he drew his inspiration for a law career and a life spent chasing dreams and dinosaurs from Seminole Public Library and the high school debate team.

"I started going to the library when I was very young; I remember filling out my first application for a library card," Whitten said. "I got interested in science fiction and almost became a scientist.

"The debate team was the biggest influence on my life. Melvin's daughters were a little older and a little younger than me and they were fantastic debaters. I chose law because of the debate team."

He grew up knowing the Moran family, who, he said, served along with Seminole resident David Boren, as his lifelong mentors.

"I remember working at my dad's used car lot and Melvin coming down," Whitten said. "I was in maybe eighth grade and I asked my dad who that was. He said, 'That is Melvin Moran, probably the nicest guy you will ever meet.'"

Melvin's support of the debate team while Whitten was in high school cemented their friendship.

Whitten went on to use Melvin as a role model when, as a successful attorney, he began his own philanthropies. He is an organizer of Pros for Africa, which brings professionals from all walks of life to Uganda to help with infrastructure needs, including building homes and medical clinics.

Whitten also organized Explorology, a program through the Sam Noble Museum of Natural History in Norman, which brings children out into the world of science, through summer workshops and archaeological digs.

"We are trying to get kids interested in science," Whitten said. "I have taken some inspiration from the Children's Museum for this. I have a strong belief that all children are like plants: if you water every plant and fertilize it and take good care of it, it will grow strong and true.

"Children are like that. If you give them something to inspire them they will get interested and succeed.

"Our country is in a real fix here," Whitten continued. "Things have changed since I was a kid. When I grew up, the U.S. was number one in science in the world. That is no longer true. Standardized testing shows we are number 34, and I think we will pay for that. We cannot let China and South Korea have all the scientists. We have to challenge our kids and get them interested in science and math and that is what the museum is good for."

So one day Whitten had lunch with Melvin at a Mexican restaurant and heard about the new science wing that could not be finished until they could afford to expand the museum.

"I was intrigued," Whitten said. "I love science and want to promote it for our children, so I made a gift to the museum."

MODIFICATION

In appreciation for his generosity, the museum board asked Whitten to name the new wing.

Because of her participation in the healthcare exhibit, Whitten named the wing, the "Kim Henry Science Works Wing."

They named the healthcare exhibit Centennial Hospital, thanks to some funding by the Oklahoma Centennial Commission, and it replaced the old hospital exhibit that had been in place since the museum's opening.

When the wing opened, a thank-you banquet at Seminole State College gave the donors a chance to see what had been done with their money, and gave the museum officials another opportunity to recognize the donors.

Old Dr. Bones, a skeleton riding a bicycle,

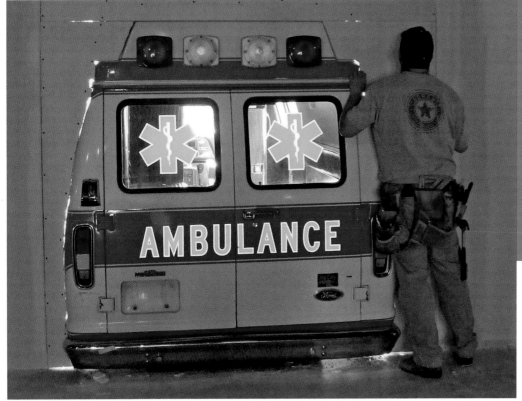

In 2008, Dale Donaho and Keith Shaw worked to secure the ambulance in the east wall of the museum.

MODIFICATION

made the cut to join the new healthcare exhibit. Marci and her husband traveled to Missouri and secured an ambulance, which was built into the east wall. Several fitness areas now show children the importance of exercise and motivate them to dance and jump. A doctor's lounge holds gowns and gloves and another exhibit lets them wash their hands, then see how well they did as they place their hands under ultra-violet light.

In the surgical suite, a glass-encased operating table holds a plastic patient, and gloved hand openings let children reach inside to pretend to "operate."

Posters show the different jobs available in the medical field. X-ray tables and a CT scanner complete the downstairs portion of the healthcare exhibit.

The stairs are lined with glass displays of surgical tools. The old tools were hard to come by, because they are often donated to Third World countries after use.

Upstairs is the hospital's "nursery" and patient room. Children tend and pat a plastic baby in an isolette. Ultra-sound pictures show the baby's development before birth.

One of the most popular exhibits in this area is called "Step into my Shoes." Visitors step into large plastic shoes, and depending on which area they select, a video is triggered which outlines a particular medical profession, what they do and the education required for the job. This exhibit tells visitors about

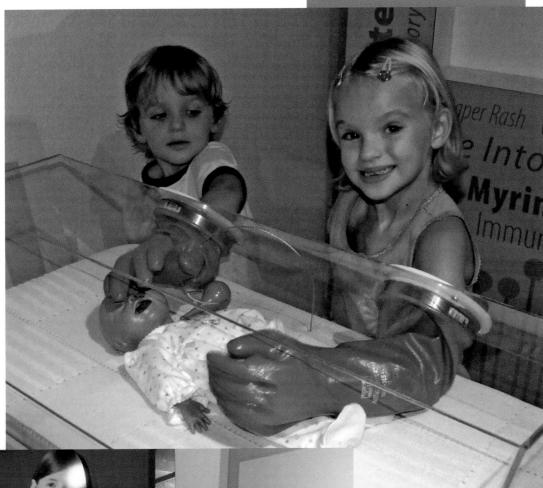

When the Kim Henry Science Works Wing opened in 2007, children and their families flocked to tend to a "preemie" in the new healthcare exhibit's nursery.

eight different medical vocations.

Across the hall is another 1,500-square foot area that currently is empty, but well used Marci said. The space eventually will be used for expansion, but for now, children enjoy it as a place to run, play, do flips and, occasionally, to sit.

In the entry to the new wing is the audio-kinetic exhibit, a favorite of both Melvin and Marci.

"I had seen some of these in museums and shopping malls," Marci said. She once gave a

The audio-kinetic exhibit is a great favorite at the museum.

presentation at a large company in Oklahoma City for an audio-kinetic exhibit and the CEO said he went into engineering because of his experience with just such an exhibit in a museum. They did not donate to the exhibit however.

"Perhaps they could not," Marci said. "The company is no longer is existence."

Marci never gave up on the idea, however, and some years later when Leilani and Dennis Roesler wanted to make a donation, she suggested the audio-kinetic exhibit. Dennis Roesler was an engineer and served as Seminole city engineer for many years.

"Dennis jumped at the opportunity to assist with funding," Marci said.

The Donahos traveled to Ithaca, New York, to meet with designer George Rhoads from Rock Stream Studios. Dale Donaho chose the components and, three years later, the current exhibit was delivered to the museum.

"Along with the Handi-Capable exhibit, the audio-kinetic exhibit is my favorite," Marci said. "I like Handi-Capable for what it can develop within people, an awareness for others, and the audio-kinetic for a 'minds-on' experience. It has a calming effect on people and certainly sparks an interest in children to predict outcomes of the rolling balls."

Melvin said it is one of the most favored and talked about exhibits in the museum. The L-shaped, glass-cased exhibit shows balls spiraling down between steel rods, bouncing into wire baskets and hitting other balls to create more movement. The exhibit was tested for 1,000 hours before even coming to the museum. The pale, neutral walls surrounding the exhibit make it a quiet, relaxing spot in the sometimes-chaos of the Children's Museum.

In the corner behind the exhibit is a painting by famous Israeli artist Yahuda Golden — an American flag shaped into a heart in honor of the museum's 10th anniversary in 2003.

The museum boasts a collection of Cherokee arrowheads and tomahawks, on permanent loan from Bill and Pat Claiborne of Tulsa. The artifacts were from around 1900 and found in the area of what is now the Oklahoma-Arkansas border. They had been in a museum that went out of business and came to the Jasmine Moran Children's Museum through Bill Claiborne's sister, Suann Shepherd. Before her death, Shepherd was Melvin's office manager.

Other later exhibits include an agricultural exhibit, an oil and gas exhibit and a dinosaur dig.

An energy exhibit, sponsored by Oklahoma Energy Resources Board, Koch Industries, Phillips Petroleum and Arkla, was planned and designed by Marilyn Moran-Townsend's company CVC Communications, working with an exhibit company. She met with OERB representatives to design the exhibit.

There children can explore oilfields by hitting gushers or dry holes on a computer. A pumping unit shows them how oil is pumped from the ground to the surface. A push of a button teaches how petroleum-based products are made.

"The exhibit has been very successful, but we now have plans to replace it with a bigger and better energy exhibit," Melvin said.

Marci said a committee will be formed to determine goals for the exhibit.

"Dale and I have an idea of what we want, but we want to include people from the field to help us," she said. "There will be a Seminole component referencing the rich history of oil in Seminole County."

Outdoors one also can find a tank battery and child-sized refinery. Funding was provided by the Oklahoma Energy Resources Board.

Marci also wanted a dinosaur "dig."

"Sonia Scott, Liz Gunter and Michelle Sneed and I came up with pictures of dinosaurs we wanted in the exhibit," she said. "We wanted a stegosaurus mold in the ground. Roberta Pales at the Stovall Museum helped Joe Robinson to cast a mold.

"The mural on the wall was the Oklahoma prairie," Marci said. I asked Teri Hooten, Marilyn Stewart and Barbara Cathey if they could turn it into a prehistoric mural and they did."

Children work to "dig" up a stegosaurus in the museum's dino dig. *Courtesy of Jacklyn Patterson Photography.*

Murals also were done by April Ledbetter Jones, Neva Cathy, Thelma Arnold and her daughter, Heather Dillon.

Doyle Morris said the eagle and the raccoon in the dinosaur area are signed Harvey Pratt originals. Pratt, a Native American, is one of the leading forensic artists in the United States, currently serving as artist for the Oklahoma State Bureau of Investigation.

Shortly after the dinosaur exhibit opened, two twin girls were sitting in an off-limits part of the exhibit. When asked to come down, they said, "It is okay, my grandfather owns this museum." They were Keith Shaw's grandchildren.

Another later exhibit was a 1928 Santa Fe caboose, which children climb on and in.

"How do you move an 80,000-pound caboose? It was found in a train yard in Kansas City and shipped by rail to Shawnee," said Keith Shaw. "Ronnie Allison brought it on a truck he usually used to haul drilling rigs."

R.D. Lozier still laughs when he talks about how he and Doyle Morris set the 1928 Santa Fe caboose on its tracks.

"They just dumped the tracks down by the barn," said the diminutive Lozier. "I wondered how we were supposed to get the tracks over there to the caboose. I asked Doyle and he just picked up one end under his arm. They were 30 feet long and weighed probably 300 pounds. I picked up the other end and he just looked at me. I said, 'Well, get

A 1928 Santa Fe caboose is a fun exhibit on which to climb, but challenged the construction team who had to haul it in and set it on tracks. *Courtesy Jacklyn Patterson Photography.*

moving, this thing is heavy.'"

Then they had to figure out how to get the tracks under the caboose. They called local wrecker truck owner Jimmy Howard and asked for a truck. Howard said he did not have a truck to do it, but promised another way.

"When he got there, he had an air compressor," Lozier said. Howard set four cushions under the caboose and pushed a button to air it up.

"We put the tracks under it and welded them and he let it down," Lozier said. "It worked perfectly."

A construction exhibit is located in a corner marked in yellow and black construction tape, filled with large rocks and trucks for hauling them. Nearby is the table of magnets and another of large dominoes for building, an original exhibit at the museum.

The Super Service Center exhibit has a car where children practice their mechanic skills. It was donated by former Oklahoma City Mayor Ron Norick and his wife, Kandy, Norick's parents and aunt; Seminole residents Jerry and Cecil Sullivan and Harvey and Pam Robinson; and Seminole industry EnviroSystems. Norick's son was a NASCAR driver, which prompted their idea for a "pit" type display. Visitors at the museum are often interested to see as many girls working on the cars with screwdrivers and drills as boys. Even adults get into the act, rolling underneath the car on a "creeper."

High above the main floor is the ultra-light plane donated by Jim Goff. The cockpit is now filled

by a fluffy "Snoopy," made by Wewoka resident Betty Cohen, who felt the plane needed a pilot. It no longer rotates, thanks to adjustments made by Lozier when the plane nearly fell on a Sunday during a peak visitor period.

Nowadays visitors can enjoy child-friendly lunches like peanut butter and jelly sandwiches, popcorn, hot dogs and nachos in the café run by the museum and brightly painted by Teri Hooten. The café, originally built to the specifications of Helen Adams, was later run by the Billy Boy Barbecue

The museum's café was built to the specifications of Helen Adams of Seminole's Lunch 'n' Such. *Courtesy Jacklyn Patterson Photography.*

owners, then later by Zora Fowler's mother, June Thorn. With only a few hours of operation a day, and most school groups bringing their own lunches, it became more feasible for the museum to take over operation themselves.

The adjoining birthday room can hold about 15, but crowds of up to 100 can celebrate in the bigger lunch room in Roesler Hall. The birthday room has been decorated and dedicated to Billie and Joe Mills by their son Roger Mills.

One of the first things children see as they enter the museum is the gravity well. A large circular table with a hole in the bottom, the exhibit is irresistible. A coin dropped will circle and circle, rolling on its edge before dropping out of sight.

"I saw one of these at the Boston Children's Museum," Melvin said. "Sunoco financed the purchase for our museum. Monies from this exhibit are considered earned revenue."

The museum is set up to allow one person to work the gift shop and sell tickets, unless an unusually large crowd is expected.

The Children's Theater, painted to look like the Royal Drury Lane Theater in London, not only serves as an orientation room for visiting school groups and plays, but has been the site of meetings for local and state boards.

Most of the original exhibits are still in place, but there have been several changes. The dollhouse built by Marilyn and Dick Fulton is still in the museum, but is now covered for viewing only.

"There used to be a drawer underneath to keep the extra pieces," Marilyn Fulton said. "But they kept disappearing."

"The plan was for children to play with the house and rearrange the furniture," Melvin said. "We soon found that was not practical so Plexiglas was placed over the house. But the rooms are fully visible to the children and the house is very much enjoyed."

The small train in the Fultons' diorama did not last long, as it kept derailing. Tiny fingers turning cranks and wheels and grown-ups moving things caused the train to break and fall apart.

"Someone was always having to put a new gear in it," Fulton said. The train was dismantled three years later.

The Bubble Factory has been completely reworked, with the rubber tractor tire replaced by steel tray and fittings fabricated by Seminole's Blue Wave Boat Company.

The classroom has changed, too. In the 1980s, when the museum was being built, the common theory was that kids needed more access to computers.

"I remember how excited we were with the schoolroom and the office, and the fact that we were able to put Macintosh computers into cabinets where they would be protected and yet the children would have access to them," said Zora Fowler, who helped plan that exhibit.

The computers, however, were short-lived. "They were so high maintenance," Marci said. "The

Melvin Moran enjoys watching the children play in the museum almost every day. He enjoys the Bubble Factory almost as much as the visitors.

kids did not know how to use them."

"Technology changed so fast, and before long kids had computers at home, so they were no longer a novelty," said Cai Levy.

Later exhibits have been based more on play, and those have proven to be the mainstay of the museum. Exhibits like Creativity Central is nearly always filled with children.

"What I think is most important about this exhibit is the opportunity it provides for adults to be kids again," Marci said.

Once Governor Frank Keating and his wife, First Lady Cathy Keating, stopped by the museum for a short visit. Both had their entourages and were on very tight schedules. Melvin took the governor on a fast tour and Marci led the first lady on a quick pass

MODIFICATION

through the museum.

"She landed in the art room and started painting a very simple design," Marci said. "When the governor turned the corner, she motioned to him and invited him to participate in painting as well."

With his security guards telling him, "Governor, we do not have time," Frank Keating was in a dilemma for only a moment. Better to please your wife than the guards, so he started to paint as well.

"They kept adding designs and different colors," Marci recalled. "Cathy encouraged him to add a little more to his painting.

"It was really special to watch two high-profile people letting down their guards and just going back to their youth."

Marci saved the couple's artwork, presenting them later during a tribute for Cathy Keating's contributions for children.

"The banquet was attended by hundreds of people," Marci said. "At the conclusion of my speech, I introduced this wonderful piece of art that we had just acquired and that it was not for sale.

"I had had it framed and it was hidden under a black velvet covering. I really built up this rare work of art. They were so delighted when I unveiled their artwork. The audience burst into applause.

"The point I was trying to make was, 'The Children's Museum is a place where children play to learn and adults learn to play,'" Marci said, quoting the museum's motto.

The Keatings' framed artwork can be seen in

the long front hall that opens into the museum's main gallery.

In February, 2004, the museum hired Betty Smith as part-time education coordinator; she recently had retired as assistant superintendent of Seminole Public Schools. She had been one of those who attended the first luncheon in 1988, and had worked on the dentist's office and Handi-Capable exhibit with former educator Bonnie Lee Grisso. After the museum opened, she volunteered on weekends. She had served on the Board of Trustees until November, 2002, when she was elected to the museum's Executive Committee.

Smith had taken her oldest grandson to the museum often from the time he was three years old. On the first visit, she said, he did not want to leave and they spent the day. After that, Smith learned to take him about two hours before closing time.

"Grandmas wear out," she explained. It was her grandchildren's favorite place to play for many years. They are now 22 and 16.

Smith's main duties as education coordinator were to develop programs and to assist with the volunteer program.

"Once when discussing the volunteer handbook with a 10-year-old potential volunteer, he said, 'You mean I cannot come and play all day wherever I want in the museum?'" Smith said.

"I knew then I did not explain it very well when I was visiting his school — or he was not listening. I told him he would be assigned to a particular exhibit, but he could help others play."

She planned, implemented and evaluated programs, which usually were held on summer Fridays or weekends.

In addition to locating, scheduling and advertising appropriate and interesting programs, she developed an art project to correlate with each month.

"Now that was a trick, since I am not at all 'artsy,'" Smith remembered. "Many times the kids' finished product looked much better than mine."

Programs were free to participants and presenters were often people Smith had known from her years in the school system. She also scoured state and local newspapers for ideas.

The goal of the programs was to expose children to educational, particularly scientific, activities that they might not otherwise have a chance to do. Most activities were hands-on.

"When each of the programs was advertised, I would put down an approximate age level," Betty said. "It was followed most of the time, but no one was turned away."

She found an origami instructor, who taught math at South Rock Creek; she came for several sessions. Each time she started with simple paper-folding designs and then progressed to more difficult projects.

Local pastor and photographer Roger Brewer gave sessions to two age groups on how to take pictures. He gave each of the 12 or so participants a disposable camera and directed them to go out into the museum and shoot. When they returned a week later, he had their pictures and critiqued their photos with praise and tips on what might be improved.

"The participants loved launching eggs on water rockets with local teacher Michele Sneed as their facilitator," Smith said. After following her instructions, the rockets were taken outside and attached to a pump, which the student operated.

"It was fun to see which one went the farthest without breaking the egg," she said. "Michele would then discuss with each one why their rocket did or did not go far."

Seminole Police Officer Terry McGinnis

During Betty Smith's tenure as education coordinator, Seminole Police Officer Terry McGinnis was invited to give a bike safety program. *Courtesy Sharon Wallace/ Seminole Producer.*

presented a bike safety program. The kindergarten through grade three participants then rode the museum's bikes through Safety Town, practicing the safety rules they had learned.

The animals from the Little River Zoo were popular, Smith said. She especially remembered the bobcat and porcupine. Students heard talks on the animals and then got to pet them. Some animals were allowed to roam free around the room.

She had the children vote during the Bush vs. Gore presidential campaign, making pictured ballots and voting booths in the theater room. The kindergarteners asked "What is a president?" Another said she could not vote because she did not know either candidate.

"I told her it was her right to vote or not vote," Smith said.

She invited a Spanish dance company from Norman to do an evening program and the public was invited.

"It was an excellent program and the costuming was fantastic," Smith said. "Those who came really enjoyed it, but we had very little participation from the community. That was a let-down because it had taken some doing and expense to get them there."

Smith developed and presented a health program about body organs using the museum's 10-foot tall stuffed doll, Stuffie. The stuffed organs could be taken out of Stuffie's zippered torso for guests to see the specific shapes and hear about

Children were fascinated by the inner workings of a huge rag doll filled with soft, stuffed organs. Stuffie zipped open for easy "surgeries." *Courtesy Jacklyn Patterson Photography.*

Two of the traveling exhibits from the Donald W. Reynolds Foundation were a Mayan exhibit in 2010, being unloaded and set up, and a Science Matters external exhibit which appealed to older students.

their functions and how to keep them healthy. The 15-minute program was offered on Wednesday, Thursday and Friday.

Once maintenance head Doyle Morris found a child completely zipped up inside Stuffie.

Smith also periodically arranged free-standing exhibits on topics like paleontology, the red-tailed hawk and the Hope Trunk items from the Oklahoma City National Memorial Museum; they were on display from a week to four weeks.

"The programs and exhibits were fun to prepare and execute," Smith remembered. "Not only were they educational for the participating students, but for me as well. Working at the museum was an enjoyable time of my life and I am grateful to have had the opportunity to try my hand at something new."

She retired in August of 2005.

In 2003, the museum was accepted into a network of traveling exhibits organized and funded by the Donald W. Reynolds Foundation.

"I was given the opportunity to make a presentation to the Reynolds

Foundation, while they were headquartered in Tulsa, and I had only three days to prepare," Melvin said. "I asked them for money for outdoor projects and they asked for cost estimates. I pulled a number out of my head: $1.5 million.

"They said, 'Sorry, we cannot help you. We do not fund anything less than $5 million.'"

The Reynolds Foundation's interest in children's museums is said to have began when the executive director visited one with his grandson. He returned to his board requesting they do more for "hands-on" museums. The foundation, with headquarters in Las Vegas, funds projects only in Oklahoma, Arkansas and Nevada.

"Representatives from the foundation interviewed me for two hours and then asked us to be a partner in the Oklahoma Museum Network," Marci said recently. "We have been part of that network now for nine years. They also have a vehicle which goes to rural areas with exhibits for children who cannot get to cities and we have had that twice, with different exhibits both times."

With the Science Museum Oklahoma in Oklahoma City, Great Plains Museum in Lawton and Leonardo's Warehouse in Enid, the Seminole museum shares in the science museum on wheels and the 60 exhibits created by the Exploratorium in San Francisco. The exhibits and the vehicle constitute a $7.2 million contribution from the Donald W. Reynolds Foundation. The exhibits rotate every six months. The Jasmine Moran Children's Museum devotes 1,500

One of the newest exhibits is a pontoon boat donated by one of Seminole's newest businesses, Blue Wave Boats. Blue Wave Boats employees assist in moving the boat in and afterwards officials, including Blue Wave owners Pam and Roger Parks, join Melvin for a photo.

square feet to the rotating Reynolds Foundation exhibits.

As the curtain closes on the museum's first 20 years, organizers were looking forward to the newest expansion and exhibit: an exact cast of a dinosaur that roamed Oklahoma 110-million years ago. The Acrocanthosaurus bones were found near Atoka, an hour and a half southeast of Seminole, in 1983. The original bones were bought by the North Carolina Museum of Natural Sciences in Raleigh; they are so fragile, only a cast is on display there. The Black Hills Institute in South Dakota has the mold and a

Contractor Keith Shaw, center, goes over plans for the museum's new front with museum director Marci Donaho and her husband Dale. *Courtesy Karen Anson.*

cast for the Jasmine Moran Children's Museum has been ordered and paid for by Reggie Whitten, the Oklahoma City attorney and self-described science lover and dinosaur buff who funded the Kim Henry Science Works Wing. The cast's construction was expected to take about six months.

"My grown-up job is legal stuff, but I dream about dinosaurs," Whitten said. He has hunted dinosaur remains in Wyoming, Black Mesa State Park in northwestern Oklahoma and in South America.

"We could have gone with a T-Rex," he added. "They are the best-known dinosaurs. But we thought we needed an Oklahoma dinosaur."

Whitten said the Acrocanthosaurus, whose original bones were named Fran after Fran Graffham of Geological Enterprises of Ardmore who bought the bones and cleaned them up, would have been tougher and scarier than any T-Rex.

"The T-Rex had a bigger head and jaws, but it had these wimpy little arms," said Reggie. "He could not even reach his mouth. They are not even sure what those arms were for.

"The Acrocanthosaurus would have been a terror because it had arms with these incredible hooks that could rip the flesh off the other dinosaurs. Its smaller head made it more agile and it was more of a threat. It would have been a terrifying monster. And the best specimen in the world was found right here. It was Oklahoma born and bred."

Other Acrocanthosaurus bones have been found in Arizona, but the only skull found, to date, was the one found in Atoka.

"You will not be able to tell that this cast is not the original bones," Whitten continued, enthusiastically.

The south-facing glass front wall of the museum will be extended out to place the giant-sized dino cast in the front windows, to be visible from SH 9 which runs in front of the museum.

"I think attendance will go up," Whitten said. "I expect the museum will be crawling with kids. I have seen pictures. It is a show-stopper."

The expansion was expected to be completed when the museum closed on Labor Day, 2012, for its annual two-week clean-up and restoration.

"This year we may shut down for three or four weeks as we will do our building construction then," Melvin said.

The new dinosaur exhibit was expected to be in place by October, 2012.

Executive Director Marci Donaho marvels at the size of the dinosaur cast expected to make its debut at the museum in October, 2012.

Reflection

reflection (ri-flek-shuhn), n. the act of reflecting or the
state of being reflected; a fixing of the thoughts
on something; careful consideration

CLOSING AN ERA, THE FIRST 20 YEARS

After 18 years at the museum, 14 as head of maintenance, Doyle Morris took medical retirement from the museum.

"In 2004, I was in the hospital for 11 days and nearly died," he said. "In September, 2006, I got sick again. I had arthritis real bad and my pancreas was acting up again. It was a struggle to go to work and I was not doing them any good. I cut back to part time, but in the end I felt I was not doing my job, so I left."

It was with a heavy heart that he left his friends and his job, and his loss was hard for the museum, too.

"I loved the people there just like family," Morris said. "Winnie Stilwell was so good with the kids [volunteers]. Phyllis Richardson, Teresa Jones, were so good."

The museum gave him a retirement breakfast and a large gift certificate for Bass Pro.

"It was a neat job," Morris said. "I knew how many screws were there and where they all went. The people who came after me did not have my same job; I made my own job because I knew so much about the building."

He was Employee of the Month four times during his tenure, although he pointed out that he never voted for himself.

Nowadays, Morris said, he always looks as he drives by and reads everything he sees about the museum, but never returns.

"It is hard to go back," he said.

In 2005 Marci was named by the Oklahoma governor to the Board of Regents for Seminole State College, which caused longtime board member Lana Reynolds to decide to step down as president of the museum's Executive Board. She had served longer than any other president besides Marci herself.

"As Executive Board president I would be setting Marci's salary and making other decisions regarding her employment," Lana said. "I decided it would be appropriate for me to step down.

"But it was a very emotional decision."

Reynolds had served on the Governing Board since its inception, and as chairman of communications for the Exhibit Design Committee in the very beginning. She was Publicity Committee chair during the period surrounding the museum's opening. She was secretary of the Executive Committee from 1996 to 2000 and was president of the Executive Board from 2002.

A letter she wrote at the time shows how she felt

about leaving the leadership position.

"It is with much sadness that I step away from this leadership role with the museum," she wrote. "It has been an honor and a privilege to be so closely involved with a great cause and with great people. I am extremely proud of the growth and development of the Jasmine Moran Children's Museum. Serving as president has been the highlight of my volunteer service to many local and state organizations over the past two decades. I will continue to be highly involved in the work of the museum through the Governing Board, through committee work and in any capacity which I am able to help."

Reynolds said Marci's addition to the SSC Board of Regents had been a real asset because of her educational background, management experience and positive personality.

"I am thrilled to be working with her for the betterment of Seminole State College," Reynolds added.

In 2007 the museum's development officer, Dr. Carmen Notaro, chose to move on.

"I am proud to have 'worked' for Melvin and Jasmine and for Seminole State College in a unique partnership that established development offices in both places at the same time," Notaro said. "It was 13 years of loving to go to work and to be inspired and challenged."

During his time working for both entities, Notaro said he saw real cooperation between the museum and college.

"The college has invested its human, physical and financial resources, even sharing donors, so that both educational institutions could prosper and flourish together in harmony for the good of the larger community," he said.

"Melvin Moran believes so much in both of these institutions and the community where they exist."

The museum has expanded eight times to nearly 40,000 square feet and 22 acres. It recently recorded 60,000 annual visitors. It has won many awards, including the 2007 Outstanding Attraction Award at the Governor's Conference on Tourism.

"The reason the Children's Museum has won national and international acclaim is because that nurturing, guidance, support and love [that Melvin gives] is a magnet for children who know it when they see it," said his daughter, Marilyn Moran-Townsend. "Dad's love for kids is very real and very alive in this amazing place."

Board member Frank Merrick became involved with the museum in 1994, having turned down Melvin's requests for donations until he moved from Ardmore to Oklahoma City and saw the museum for the first time.

"I was very much impressed," he remembered. "My first reaction was to fund a trip for Ardmore school kids to come to the museum."

He was asked to serve on the board and continues to serve nearly 20 years later.

Merrick is proud of the continuing support that his family's Merrick Foundation and his company, Foundation Management Inc., which helps non-profits, have been able to provide.

In addition to his work, Merrick has supported the museum personally with his time and money because, he said, of Melvin and Jasmine and Marci.

"You will not find a bigger heart than Melvin's," he said. "And there has not been anything done at the museum that Jasmine was not involved in. She may not always be front and center, but she is at work behind the scenes."

Asked what, of all the ways he had supported the museum, did he believe had been the most beneficial, Frank said, "I am most proud of the money we have given and what they have done with it."

He also cited the input he has been able to provide from the aspect of the board.

"I got a lot more than I ever gave," he said. "I have met a lot of nice people, been able to see first hand a well-run organization and I personally have gained from my association with Melvin and the executive board."

And he believes, as his grandchildren come of age, he will be enjoying his connection with the museum even more.

"I remember the first time I met Melvin Moran," said Oklahoma First Lady Kim Henry. Her husband's family had been close to the Moran family for a long time.

"My father-in-law had such tremendous respect for Melvin," she said. She met Melvin at the first dinner for the museum.

"Melvin was just as delightful as my father-in-law

said he was," she said. "There were a lot of people there who gave a lot of money to help the museum get started.

"Brad [former Governor Brad Henry] and I were just married, still young. He was in law school and we did not have any money to give to the museum. But you would not have known that by the way Melvin treated us. He treated everyone the same, large donor or not. It is an incredible characteristic.

"When we left, I turned to Brad and said, 'Did your father give him a lot of money in our name?' and he said no. I was amazed. Melvin was just so warm. He makes everyone feel at home. Melvin has such passion, such integrity and character and, because of that, everyone got on board. You just want to help him. His enthusiasm is infectious. He is definitely a rare individual."

Similarly, the former governor's cousin, Robert Henry, helped out with a donation to the museum.

"I did not have the kind of money some people have, but I had some I wanted to give," he said. "Melvin said, 'Here's what we have a need for: give this money instead to create a little scholarship fund to pay the small entrance fee that we will have for kids who cannot afford it at all.' That was a great idea. The next time he was talking about the museum to a group, he said, 'Attorney General Henry established this scholarship,' giving all the credit to me for the modest contribution I made. That is Melvin Moran for you."

Kim Henry cites the museum's success as proof of Melvin's enthusiasm and ability to inspire others to do good works. "The museum inspires creativity and imagination," she said. "Children go into the museum and see opportunity and learn work ethics. They play in the grocery store; they crawl into the airplane cockpit, it inspires a lifelong love. They get so caught up in imagination they do not realize how much they are learning.

"And if we fire creativity and imagination, it teaches children divergent thinking. I do think you can teach creativity — oh, not to be a Da Vinci or a Mozart — but you can teach creative thought, thinking outside the box, analytical thinking. And that makes kids more successful in education and in life."

Reggie Whitten, credited with funding the Kim Henry Science Works Wing and the new Acrocantho-saurus exhibit, said the museum has earned a place in Oklahoma history.

"I have been to children's museums in Dallas and Chicago," he said. "The Jasmine Moran Children's Museum is better than both of them by far. It is hard for some people to believe there is a museum of that quality here. We are so blessed to have these people [Melvin and Jasmine] to do this for us. Our children are so much better off for it."

Whitten also serves on the museum's Board of Trustees, and said that he would continue to support the museum in any way he could.

"I think museums are like incubators," he said. "They incubate the mind, stimulate it. I think that, as a community and a state, we owe it to the children of Oklahoma to keep the museum alive and I will always do my part."

Destination

destination (des-tuh-ney-shuhn), n. the place to which a person or thing travels or is sent; the purpose for which something is destined.

On the occasional day when there are only a few children in the museum, quiet play is possible. But on most days, as schools bus their students for field trips, the museum is crowded, loud and rambunctious, colorful and high energy, just like the children themselves, and as vital as a waterfall. Even the parents will bang the gavel in the courtroom exhibit. The children climb on everything stationary, stack foam blocks higher than their heads, and when the blocks fall, they jump on them. They pose for pictures, then run on to the next exhibit. In Creativity Central, the children color, cut, glue and paint.

The grocery store is one of the busiest areas, with children pushing shopping carts through aisles of real and pretend cans, boxes and produce, then checking out on the store's cash register. At the end, they are encouraged to return their purchases to the shelves for the next shopper.

Longtime staff member Tony Lenora helps little Abigail Pauls of Seminole at the fire pole. *Courtesy Karen Anson.*

"Maybe I need to re-evaluate my shopping skills," joked one mother, watching her daughter return her purchases to the shelves.

Most days there is a solid line for the fire pole, and each child must jump into the fire truck to try the buttons and dials, the steering wheel and the horn.

"Springtime can be like a war zone here," Marci said. "Imagine 400 to 500 visitors, mostly little ones, running around having a great time. It can be extremely tiring and testing of your good humor. That is where our museum soldiers – our staff – come in. Whether they are opening the doors to

100 screaming children who have come 30 minutes early, answering three phone lines while working on financials or updating the membership list, or working in a café with the air conditioning testing their faith, they do it with style and grace and, all the while, with smiles. Our staff is amazing."

After much experience, the museum tries to book only 300 children at a time, because they will be accompanied by nearly half that number of adults. But with several time slots in a day, there can be 800 to 900 visitors a day.

Nearly twenty years after the museum opened, however, the anchor exhibits — bubbles, magnets, shadowbox — still receive the most traffic.

"It is neat to see adults and children setting up dominoes to fall," Marci said. "Less is more. The old exhibits are tried and true. It is all about play."

Staff and volunteers wear radios to keep track of where everyone is and needs to be. Each week one of three employees serve as floor supervisor, making assignments as needed. They tell hilarious stories about their work.

"Once I kept hearing this kid saying he was going to play in the shower," said Tammy Duck, a floor supervisor and self-described, "big kid."

"I thought I better follow him and found he meant the bubble machine."

Dorilla DeLoach, a tiny Ecuadorian who retired after more than 22 years at Wrangler, has filled her days at the museum since 2001. Few guess her age at 70, so quick and active is she.

"I no like to slow down," she said in her heavily-accented English. "If I slow down, it is better He takes me."

If she sees something broken, sometimes she will have it fixed before the maintenance department even arrives. She is one of the most dependable and enthusiastic employees.

"One time, a little one, he say to his mother, 'I like to play here. More I like this lady,'" DeLoach said. "His mother was so embarrassed. He asked if he can give me a hug and he hugged me so tight! Now every time he comes, he says, 'You are my special friend.'"

Tiny Ecuadorian Dorilla DeLoach, 70, has worked at the museum since 2001. She helps Brandi and Brian Adams' children, Ava and Marin, make masks in Creativity Central. *Courtesy Karen Anson.*

It is no wonder the children love her. She smiles constantly and says, "Hello, sweetie," to almost everyone. Her favorite place to work is at Creativity Central, even though that often means cleaning up spilled paint and scrubbing crayon marks off tables and floors. She also runs the train, does announcements and pitches in wherever she is needed.

The museum's constant focus on tolerance and diversity is a lesson needed in the world, and sometimes even in a place of fun and education like a children's museum. DeLoach has, on several occasions, had parents tell her to stay away from their children and make racial slurs because of her brown skin. Asked her response, she says she smiles and says "Okay, I am sorry," but has found herself crying about it later.

Melvin, at 82, is at the museum every single day.

"He goes out on the floor, reads the guest book, visits with people," Marci said. "He asks where they are from and how they found out about the museum."

His schedule has him at the museum mid- to late-morning but always before lunch. Because Melvin is at the museum every day, Marci and he have developed a very close professional and social friendship.

"I can joke with Melvin, tell him things I cannot tell anyone else," she said. "Sometimes we agree to disagree. If he does not get his way, he will say,

'Marci, I will have to trust your judgment,' but he will go to the nth degree to change my mind. If he still does not get his way, he is a gentleman and accepts it. But that does not happen often. He does not allow himself to go to a negative place. If he feels strongly about something, he will trudge on to get his way. And he is usually right. It is never 'all about me,' but all about what is best."

Is Melvin her boss? Marci said she has 15 bosses — the museum's executive board. "The person in this office has to run the museum. Though most people think so, I do not consider Melvin my boss," she said. "I consider him the deputy museum director. He just gives me ideas and trusts my judgment."

After 20 years, there are now about 250 children's museums in the United States, of which the Seminole facility is one of the largest, with buildings and land holdings, even though it is located in Seminole, probably the smallest town to host a children's museum.

"The annual attendance of the Flint museum was 20,000," Melvin said. "That was our goal. But now our average annual attendance is over 55,000, and includes visitors from every community in Oklahoma, every state and 85 countries that we have documented."

The museum has had seven entities donate more than $250,000, 19 donate over $100,000, and 20 donate $50,000 or more. Since opening, the donations have totaled more than $10 million.

In addition to being named the Top Attraction

in Oklahoma at the 2007 Governor's Conference on Tourism, the museum was given the Gem Award by the American Automobile Association as one of the two top attractions in the Oklahoma, Missouri, Kansas and Arkansas tour book, sharing the honor with the Science Museum in Wichita, Kansas.

It was one of Rand McNally's 50 Hidden Gems in America and presented the David Boren Community Service Award from the Seminole Chamber of Commerce several times.

Frontier Country Marketing Association named the museum the 2004 Top Attraction and the museum was presented the Oklahoma Institute for Child Advocacy's highest award, the "Friend of Children" award.

In 2007, Marci was named Tourism Professional of the Year at the Governor's Conference on Tourism.

The Oklahoma Center for Non-Profits awarded the museum first place in "Excellence in Management" and, in 2008, gave it the Excellence Award, their highest honor in the fields of Arts and Humanities.

In 2009, the museum was recognized as runner-up for Outstanding Children's attraction by Frontier Country Marketing Association.

In 1997, Melvin was inducted into the Oklahoma Hall of Fame, and in February, 2012, he was presented a Lifetime Achievement award by Leadership Oklahoma because of his work with the museum and the state's petroleum industry. The award recognizes individuals who have used their leadership abilities to improve the quality of life for Oklahoma's citizens and its future generations.

The museum's annual budget is $700,000. Each year the Children's Museum begins with a balanced budget, and it has stayed within budget almost every year. The museum's earned income is 74 percent of expenses.

"Initially, we were disappointed because our goal was to have our income cover 100 percent of our expenses," Melvin said. "But we have since been advised by financial consultants that, for most museums, earned income is approximately 20 to 25 percent of expenses. And that, at 74 percent, we are undoubtedly in the top one percent."

The remaining 26 percent of the museum's budget comes from donations, one fundraiser a year and income from donated oil and gas royalties.

"The oil and gas royalties came about when my brother, Sidney Moran, located a package of oil and gas royalties for sale," Melvin said.

The package was bought and divided among a dozen or more individuals, but, while the investment was profitable, the paperwork required from the many different properties was "nightmarish," Melvin said.

"So many of these folks donated their oil and gas royalties to the Children's Museum," he added.

Melvin's fundraising tactic of securing well-known, well-thought-of people for his board still works.

Since the museum opened, every First Lady

of Oklahoma has served on either the Governing Board or Advisory Board. Presidents of Seminole State College, East Central University, the University of Central Oklahoma, Oklahoma City University, the University of Oklahoma, Oklahoma State University and Oklahoma State University-Oklahoma City also serve on the museum's boards, as well as the Chancellor of Higher Education.

Elected officials on the board, past and present, include the sitting governor, three former governors, one former United States senator, the speaker of the House of Representatives, one congressman, one former lieutenant governor, two former state treasurers, two former attorney generals, one former superintendent of public instruction and five present or former state legislators.

When Molly Boren asked Jasmine to serve as a board member of the Oklahoma Arts Institute, she met Chairman Ted d'Andriole. His first words to her were, "Ah, new blood! I would like for you to serve on one of our committees."

"Only if you will agree to serve on the Governing Board of the Children's Museum," she countered.

He agreed and later introduced the Morans to the Southwestern Bell president, who also agreed to serve on the museum's board of directors, a liaison that has been extremely beneficial to the museum.

"During all these years, each time a Southwestern Bell/AT&T president has been transferred, he or she encouraged his or her successor to join the board of the Children's Museum," Melvin said. "And every one has agreed.

"Our board meetings and events give Seminole people an opportunity to meet and interact with many of Oklahoma's highest profile people on a personal basis," Melvin continued.

"And it gives Oklahoma's high profile people an opportunity to know many of Seminole's extraordinary people."

The museum also contributes toward its community through employment, sales taxes on admissions and gift shop sales, and on purchases made by its visitors in other stores and restaurants. The museum also is used as an economic development tool.

The original board has grown into three boards: the Executive Board includes 15 people; the Advisory Board consists of 25 people and the Board of Trustees has a roster of 80.

Zora Fowler, who became involved in the museum early enough to scrape oil from floors in the old Power Transmission Building, and stayed long enough to serve several months as interim director, has long since moved from Seminole.

"But Jim [her husband] and I were privileged to visit the museum when we returned for a wedding in the spring of 2009," Fowler said. "We were very impressed with the evolution of the original exhibits and with all the amazing new opportunities children now have when visiting the museum. Seminole is very fortunate to have such an outstanding museum."

Cai Levy, still involved in the museum 20 years after she first marked her children's handprints on every visible wall, is still moved when she thinks about the project.

"The Morans are so charismatic and generous," she said. "Jasmine is so humble; what a wonderful legacy this is to her. And to think it might not have happened.

"I have seen Melvin watching children load groceries in the Homeland exhibit and you should have seen the look of pleasure on his face. They get so much joy from giving to others. How can you not be touched by that?"

No one could have imagined the scope of the Morans' project, nor the growth it has seen. But all those involved are still proud 20 years later of whatever they contributed and they all still seem to feel a real ownership.

"I was down at Eufaula one year and I had waded out into the water," said R.D. Lozier, who worked on the museum from demolition of the old Power Transmission building through the opening of the museum.

"I got to visiting with this lady from California and I mentioned being from Seminole. She said, 'Oh, my daughter and I love your museum.' I told her that, in one way of speaking, it really was my museum."

Anticipation

anticipation (an-tis-uh-pey-shuhn), n. realization in
advance; expectation or hope; the act of anticipating
or the state of being anticipated.

THE FUTURE

What does the future hold for the Jasmine Moran Children's Museum? Among other things, the director hopes someday to build an outdoor classroom, where teachers could bring their class for a daytrip to study plants or track animals.

"It could be like the Camp Goddard curriculum," Marci said.

"Charles B. Goddard, the founder of Camp Goddard, was a lot like Melvin," said Keith Shaw, who has been project manager for every expansion since the museum began. "He would drive up from Dallas in a station wagon and start unloading things. Camp Goddard was his dream; he loved children. It came to be in a similar way to the Children's Museum."

"I have always thought kids could be assigned a plot of land, plant seeds, then go online in their classrooms or at home to see how their plot is doing," said Dale Donaho, but Marci groans when she thinks about the administration of the idea.

At one time, the west side of the museum was planned as "Jasmine's Prairie," but became almost a museum in itself.

"A group of people led by Marie Dawson and Marilyn Stewart told us we had a treasure of special plants that do not grow anywhere else in Oklahoma," Marci said. "They would come up and photograph flowers.

"We later figured out they may have come to be there because the oil museum [located west of the Children's Museum] would have a circus fundraiser every spring. We think the circus left a lot of residue and that's how the flowers got there."

Once one of the conservationists came up when Shaw was trying to divert water with a backhoe. After an exchange of words between her and the backhoe driver, there has been little work in the area, but plans for the outdoor classroom will be a priority, Marci has said.

In 2007, Marci told the museum board that she would retire in two years. She has already headed the museum longer than any other major museum director in the state.

"I wanted them to think about getting someone in to shadow me for six months or a year," she said.

But by the end of the day: "I was just sick," she said. "I cannot retire from this place. I cannot sit at home and watch the good stuff going on here without me."

She talked to her husband, Dale, who recommended going to Melvin about how she felt and, after about two weeks of agonizing, she did.

"That is the best news I have ever heard," Melvin told her.

Both she and Melvin worry about the museum's future when both of them are no longer around to nurture it.

"Right now we are THE children's museum of Oklahoma," Marci said. "I worry about when we no longer have the physical presence of Melvin Moran around to open doors. I am 65; if God gives me 20 more years, I will still be here.

"But it will be a challenge to find someone new with this passion," she continued. "You cannot train it. I do not know anyone else who has it, besides Dale. You cannot expect others to have it just because we do. Dale's seen it through our eyes, but there are not many others. The next person will see it as a business and that is not bad, but it could change the culture. The next person will not feel all corny and mushy about this like we do."

"When something happens to Melvin, the transition will be hard," agreed board member Frank Merrick. "They have a dedicated board of good people and hopefully Marci will find board members to step up and take that leadership role."

Worries about how many children's museums are opening up across the U.S. do not concern Merrick, who works with non-profits every day.

"There are not that many really successful

children's museums in Oklahoma," he said. "I think [the Jasmine Moran Children's Museum] understands the competitiveness and I think they will live up to it."

Lana Reynolds agrees.

"Melvin and Marci are highly flattered when people come looking to duplicate the success of the museum," she said. "I think they believe that when the tide rises, we all rise. More museums will get people used to taking their children to museums.

"We will just always be the biggest and the best."

To that end, the museum's board has been working hard to build a foundation nest egg that will fund the museum's operation into perpetuity.

A few years ago, the museum board had a retreat at St. Crispin's Lodge in Seminole County. The facilitator complimented the board on the museum's financial success, then added, "When you leave St. Crispin's today and head back to Seminole, what would happen to the museum if Marci and Melvin were killed in a car accident?"

"Having persons speak openly of my demise was frightening and shocking," Melvin said. "I had not thought about the future of the museum in that regard before.

"After thinking it over, the facilitator had a very valid point. It was after that retreat that we decided we must have an endowment fund and the fund must be large enough to generate the income that would take care of the 26 percent that we were lacking to meet our expenses."

Immediately the board began an endowment fund drive. With the encouragement of their development officer, Dr. Carmen Notaro, the museum board came up with the idea of a legacy plan. They prepared pledge cards and asked the board to donate on a monthly basis — any amount from $5 up.

"This plan was a huge success," Melvin said. "A large number of our board members subscribed to the plan and we raised a significant amount of money."

Their initial goal was $1.5 million. The next goal was $2.7 million. In 2011, the endowment fund stood at about $3.5 million. The largest donor to the endowment fund was the Sarkeys Foundation with a total of $700,000. Board member Ann Alspaugh donated over $100,000.

"When the fund exceeds $5 million, we will feel secure about the future," Melvin said.

When asked "to what do you attribute the success of the Children's Museum," Melvin always credits the executive director, the staff, the volunteers and board, as well as the community.

"Our president and executive director Marci Donaho is an amazing woman," he said. "In addition to her executive director duties, she serves as the marketing director, the exhibit/decision person, and she is a major fundraiser. She is outstanding with each of these responsibilities. We are so blessed to have both Marci and her husband, Dale."

The museum's staff is composed of fifteen

dedicated and caring men and women and each staff person loves children. The volunteers range from ten-year-old children to senior citizens; Melvin believes the museum could not survive without any of them.

"Our wonderful trustees and directors, who reside in cities throughout Oklahoma, have generously given us their time, their names, their money and their valuable advice and leadership," Melvin continued.

He pointed out that donations come from scores of Oklahoma foundations, hundreds of companies and corporations, and a very large number of individuals who reside throughout Oklahoma.

"Significant donations have been bestowed on this museum in Seminole, Oklahoma," Melvin said. "This generosity was because our donors wanted to encourage children to learn, play and think about a future vocation or career.

"And we are indebted to our former superb grant writer, Carmen Notaro."

Melvin commended the Seminole community, which unconditionally embraced the museum.

"Hundreds have helped build exhibits, served as trustees and directors, served as volunteers, and helped us in every imaginable way," he said. "This is especially true of Seminole State College and Seminole Public Schools. When we go to them with a need, they always say 'yes' before we even name the request."

The museum's primary customers are the children; Melvin and the other museum advocates watch them as they learn.

"Their smiles and laughter keep us going and encourage us to continually think about how and what we can do better," Melvin said.

The Morans also credit their own children, Marilyn, Elisa and David, as encouraging them and providing exhibit construction, creative ideas and donations.

"Marci has often said that she believes that G-d wanted this museum created for children," Melvin said. "I truly believe that. Indeed, G-d has led us every step of the way.

"The creation of the Jasmine Moran Children's Museum was an impossible dream. But that dream has been fulfilled."

ANTICIPATION

Epilogue

The Jeremy and Sabrina Prince family of Yale, Oklahoma, with Jasmine and Melvin Moran, the 1-millionth visitor to enter the museum. *Courtesy Lesley Werner/Seminole Producer.*

A circus atmosphere filled the Jasmine Moran Children's Museum as the sign out front proclaimed, "Our 1 Millionth Visitor Arrives Today."

The museum was packed with spring breakers and their parents and no doubt some who hoped to be the millionth visitor and win the "very nice" prizes that founders Jasmine and Melvin Moran had been planning.

The parking lot was full and the lobby was full of children, parents, staff, media and museum board members.

As the exciting moment drew near, director Marci Donaho cleared the lobby for the photographers, sending all those waiting to pay into the museum for free.

Then she stood in the door and welcomed the 1-millionth guest, a family of five just arriving on the front porch.

"You are our millionth visitor," she said as cameras flashed and confetti flew into the air and poured down over the family.

The Jeremy and Sabrina Prince family of Yale — Johnny, five; Frank, four; and Abigail, one month old — clearly were surprised by the welcome.

It was their first time to the museum.

"We had planned to come one day during spring break and I had today off," said Jeremy, who is an aerospace engineer at Nordam in Tulsa.

Wife Sabrina operates a marriage counseling business in Stillwater.

As surprised as they were by the welcome, they were even more overwhelmed by the gifts:

- A one-year membership in the museum consortium, which also includes the Science Museum in Oklahoma City, Tulsa's Air and Space Museum, Leonardo's Children's Museum in Enid and the Museum of the Great Plains in Lawton.
- A two-night stay at any of the state parks with lodge rooms or cabins, compliments of the Oklahoma State Parks, a division of the Oklahoma Tourism and Recreation Department.
- An AT&T game and membership cards
- A gift basket from the Chickasaw Nation
- A museum gift shop basket
- Their name on a street sign in the museum's Safety Town

• And, last but not least, a four-day trip to Disney World.

"We know where that is!" said five-year-old Johnny. "It is in Florida!"

The family stood for photos in front of a huge balloon arch and a sign proclaiming them as the millionth visitor.

They chatted with the director and the founders, Melvin and Jasmine Moran.

They were interviewed by newspaper and television reporters, and finally given a chance to go play before they enjoyed a huge cake in the museum's maze area.

"This is so cool," said longtime board member Donna Hardin. "We never knew when we started working on this how well it would all turn out."

"We are so proud," said Melvin.

"We have been waiting for your family for a long time," said Marci.

The Prince Family enjoying the trip to Disney World they received as Jasmine Moran Children's Museum's one-millionth guest.

Jasmine Award Winners

PERSONS WHO HAVE ACCOMPLISHED MUCH FOR OKLAHOMA YOUTH

1999
Cathy Keating

2001
David and Molly Boren

2003
H.E. Gene Rainbolt

2005
Kim Henry

2007
Donna and George Nigh

2009
Barry Switzer

2011
Robert Henry

Foundation Benefactor Awards

1999 – J.E. and L.E. Mabee Foundation, Ronald McDonald House
Charities and the Sarkeys Foundation.
2001 – Kirkpatrick Foundation and the Noble Foundation
2003 – Merrick Foundation and Anne and Henry Zarrow Foundation
2005 – Kirkpatrick Family Fund and Robert S. and Grayce B. Kerr Foundation
2007 – The McCasland Foundation and the Sam Viersen Family Foundation
2009 – Whitten-Newman Foundation
2011 – Donald W. Reynolds Foundation and the Jearl Smart Foundation

Corporate Benefactor Awards

1999 – Koch Industries and Southwestern Bell
2001 – Cox Communications and the Oklahoma Energy Resources Board
2003 – Sonic Corporation and ConocoPhillips
2005 – BancFirst and Chesapeake Energy
2007 – OG&E and Austin Companies
2009 – Saint Francis Health Care System, Mercy Health System of Oklahoma,
Integris Health, OU Medical Center and SSM Health of Oklahoma
2011 – AEP-PSO

Special Benefactor Awards

2003 – Seminole State College and Gordon Cooper
Technology Center
2005 – Kenneth and Rose Henderson and Dennis and Leilani Roesler
2007 – Oklahoma Centennial Commission and Betty Price
2009 – Ann Alspaugh
2011 – Mike Dundee, Harry Coates and Dale Donaho

Timeline

August, 1988 — Morans discovered Flint, Michigan, museum

October, 1988 — Melvin's surprise lunch; 15 invited and attended; Marci Donaho named president of board

October 25, 1988 — The five-member executive committee met in the offices of the Chamber of Commerce, temporarily established as headquarters for the museum. At that time, the JMCM was established as a non-profit, nonreligious, tax-exempt corporation.

November 3, 1988 — A 36-member volunteer governing board of directors was elected to set administrative policy for the museum. Twenty-two prominent leaders around the state were appointed to the museum's Advisory Board.

November 22, 1988 — The museum received its Certificate of Incorporation signed by the Secretary of State of Oklahoma.

December 3, 1988 — The foundation accepted a logo designed by local illustrator Teri Hooten and adopted a formal statement of purpose for the museum.

January 10, 1989 — The board appointed Tommy Mills part-time executive director to oversee the daily business of the museum.

February, 1989 — A 20,000 square-foot facility located on a 10-acre site at 1714 State Highway 9 West [formerly the Power Transmission Building] was selected to house the museum.

February 16, 1989 — Seventeen exhibit committees were organized to research potential exhibits, and when possible, begin construction.

March 1989 — The foundation hired Carol Morrisseau Holmes and Associates as fundraising consultants to locate and identify possible funding sources for the museum.

April 14, 1989 — The foundation received notification of tax-exemption from the Internal Revenue Service.

November, 1989 — The museum's sign was erected at the site chosen for the museum. Cost was $6,235.

March, 1992 — Construction was begun.

December, 1992 — The museum's volunteer program initiated.

January 23, 1993 — Museum opens with core exhibits: courtroom, Bubble Room, Video Magic, Shadow Box Room, Infunity Mirror Room, Handi-Capable, aquarium, Homeland, Kid Town Fire Station, Creativity Central, hospital, Kermie, classroom, hand puppet theater, 1921 Model T, Tot Spot, Convair cockpit, Gentle Dental, model train, doll house, domino and magnet tables, kaleidoscope and piano keyboard on the floor. Guest speakers were Sandy Garrett and David Boren. Later exhibits include dinosaur exhibit, agriculture, oil and gas.

1995 — Dr. Carmen Notaro hired as grants writer and first egg hunt.

January 1996 — Tommy Mills leaves position of museum director; Zora Fowler begins six months as part-time director.

June, 1996 — Marci Donaho ends presidency on board; had been president since March 1988. Is hired as executive director.

1997 — Museum purchased additional seven and one-half acres northwest of building.

1998 — First golf tournament fundraiser.

1999 — First Jasmine Award presented to First Lady Cathy Keating. First Foundation Benefactor awards went to the Mabee Foundation, Ronald McDonald House Charities and the Sarkeys Foundation. Corporate Benefactor award recipients were Koch Industries and Southwestern Bell.

2000 — Additional parking lot paid for by Noble Foundation of Ardmore. Sarkeys Foundation added $250,000 to endowment.

2001 — Purchased adjoining acreages; now have 23 acres. St. Crispin's retreat, started endowment fund.

2003 — 10th anniversary in Haney Center at Seminole State College, with George Nigh as featured speaker. Brad Henry's inaugural events held at the museum in January. Honored Gene Rainbolt with Jasmine Award in Tulsa. Installed elaborate new playground equipment.

2004 — Betty Smith hired as education coordinator.

2005 — OG&E donated land to expand parking lot to the east. Betty Smith retires.

2006 — Parking lot expanded.

2007 — Welcomed 800,000th visitor. Selected for Oklahoma Museum Network. Doyle Morris retires, having worked there 18 years, 14 as head of maintenance.

2009 — Now have 38,000 square feet inside and 12 acres outside. New Norick Service Center opens.

2012 — Museum's front expanded to make room of cast of Acrocanthosaurus, donated by Reggie Whitten.

Expansions:

1 — 1993— Lunchroom

2 — 1999 — Roesler Hall, 6,000 square feet added with seed money from Dennis and Leilani Roesler

3 — 1999 — Climbing Maze, purchased with funding by Ronald McDonald House Charities, and Waterworks.

4 — 2000 — Small train and Jasmine's Ark

5 — 2001 — New train, SuperSonic Express and Safety Town, completed in 2002. The town and tracks were funded by a Department of Transportation T-21 grant and the train was funded by Sonic. Also part of this expansion was Henderson Nature Park, completed in 2003.

6 — 2006 — Castle Maze, ribbon cutting July 2, was funded by the Timmerman Family and the Oklahoma Centennial Commission – 12,000 square feet.

7 — 2007 — Kim Henry Science Works Wing, 8,400 square foot of construction completed in 2008, which includes the Heath Care exhibit, spearheaded by Kim Henry and Stan Hupfeld, who challenged other hospitals to be part of the expansion. The Whitten Newman Foundation was the single largest funder of the Kim Henry Science Works Wing. The wing also includes the audio-kinetic exhibit, built in 2007, with half the funding by the Roeslers.

8 — 2012 — Expansion of the lobby and introduction of the Acrocanthosaurus dinosaur cast.

Advisory Board officers in 2012 include Bob Jones, Marci Donaho, Jim Smart, Kenneth Henderson and, not pictured, Roger Nansel. *Photo Courtesy Karen Anson.*

Jasmine Moran with Tupper the Clown at a recent museum event.

Seminole oil entrepreneur Bill Parks, right, celebrated his 80th birthday by inviting the children of the Tipton Children's Home to the Jasmine Moran Children's Museum. Parks was the father-in-law of then director Tommy Mills.

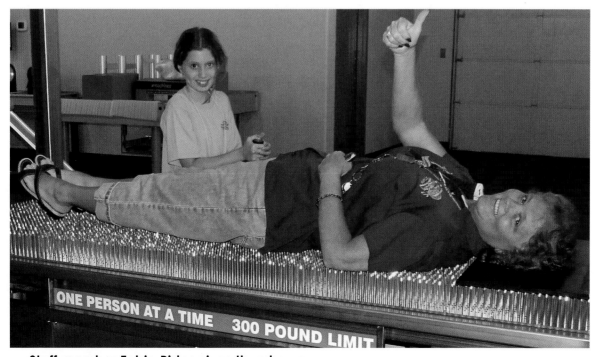

ONE PERSON AT A TIME   300 POUND LIMIT

Staff member Tobie Rider gives thumbs up while trying out a recent bed of nails exhibit.

The museum's
main gallery from a
second floor window.

Exhibit facilitators Sara Moore and Tammy Duck help young shoppers Levi Pauls, Bodey Sloan and Abigail Pauls in the Homeland grocery. *Courtesy Karen Anson.*

Paula Anderson, accounts receivables clerk, has worked for the museum for 10 years, half of the museum's lifetime. *Courtesy Karen Anson.*

At the end of 20 years, the staff of the Jasmine Moran Children's Museum includes, left to right, Mark Hallum, Sara Moore, Tammy Duck, Jennifer Cheatham Mattson, Dorilla DeLoach, Tony Lenora, Margaret Smith, Manette Mansell, Paula Anderson and Bob Bush. Not pictured are Marci Donaho and Tobie Rider. *Courtesy Karen Anson.*

PHOTO ALBUM

Manette Mansell serves as the director's administrative assistant. *Courtesy Karen Anson.*

At the museum's 20th anniversary, Margaret Smith served as cafe manager. *Courtesy Karen Anson.*

Construction begins to expand the museum's lobby to make room for the new dinosaur bone cast. *Courtesy Karen Anson.*

April Ledbetter Jones, whose work is seen throughout the museum, was called into service again, creating and painting the museum's new front. *Courtesy Karen Anson.*

**April Ledbetter Jones paints the mural which will frame
the museum's new entrance.** *Courtesy Karen Anson.*

April LedbetterJones comes down from the top of the museum to get a look at the big picture on September 21, 2012. *Courtesy Karen Anson.*